AT THE FLASH & AT THE BACI

From Sydney, Ken Bolton has lived in Adelaide since 1982 and is associated there with the Experimental Art Foundation. He writes poetry and art criticism and is publisher of Little Esther books. His major collections prior to *At The Flash & At The Baci* are a *Selected Poems* from Penguin, and *Untimely Meditations*, Wakefield Press.

Other books by Ken Bolton

Poetry
Four Poems
Blonde and French
Christ's Entry into Brussels or Ode to the Three Stooges
Two Sestinas
Talking To You
Blazing Shoes
Notes For Poems
Two Poems—A Drawing of the Sky
Sestina To The Centre Of The Brain
Selected Poems
'Untimely Meditations' & other poems
Happy Accidents
August 6th
Horizon
Three Poems For John Forbes
Europe

Art Criticism
Michelle Nikou

As editor
Homage To John Forbes

In collaboration
— with John Jenkins —
Airborne Dogs
The Ferrara Poems
The Gutman Variations
The Wallah Group
Nutters Without Fetters
Poems Of Relative Unlikelihood

AT THE FLASH & AT THE BACI

KEN BOLTON

Wakefield Press

Wakefield Press
1 The Parade West
Kent Town
South Australia 5067
www.wakefieldpress.com.au

First published 2006

Cover designed by M. Grimm for Shocking Looking Books
Typeset by Ryan Paine, Wakefield Press
Printed and bound by Hyde Park Press

National Library of Australia
Cataloguing-in-publication entry

Bolton, Ken, 1949– .
At the flash & at the baci: poems.

ISBN 1 86254 692 4.

I. Title.

A821.3

For Cath, Anna & Gabe

Many of these poems were begun, or worked on
— in the mornings before work, or in workday lunch breaks —
at the establishment which lends the collection its name,
The Flash, and at The Baci and Tu Dish,
all of them coffee shops in Adelaide's Hindley Street.
My presence certainly didn't make these places more glamorous
. . . though they had some glamour of their own.
My gratitude to the people behind their counters over the years.

Acknowledgements

Cover images from Andrew Petrusevics: *Andy P sitting in the Ginza Cafe*, 1988

Illustrating the 'Three poems for John Forbes' are: a photocopy of a newspaper reproduction of Philip Guston's painting 'Smoking, 1'; a photograph by Weegee, 'Girls watching movie, Palace Theater', c. 1943; and a photograph, 'Muddy Waters Relaxing Between Gigs', by Val Wilmer.

Rumori, Long Distance Information, Tiepolo and Holden Song were written while on a Literature Board Fellowship in the BR Whiting Studio in Rome in 2000.

Thanks to the editors involved below

Hometown, A Picture, Coffee & John Forbes Poem,
and A Prospect of the Young KB appeared first in *HEAT*,
Prospect also appeared in *Best Australian Poems 2003*
News of the Day first appeared in *Overland*
An illustrated Giles Auty Furioso was shown at the Contemporary Art Centre of South
Australia and appeared in on-line magazine *Natural Selection*
Walk on the Wild Side first appeared in *Overland* and
Walking Down from the Star Grocery in *Untimely Meditations*
Hometown & Walking Down from the Star Grocery appeared in the UK in *Shearsman*
To Generalize appeared in *The Famous Reporter* and *The Mad Hatter Review*
Two Portraits, Hindley Street Today, Horizon, Good Friday at the EAF and
poem (the ice in my glass) appeared in *JACKET*
Hi, John & Cat-bag poem in *Southerly*
Catching Up With Kurt Brereton in *Newcastle Prize Anthology*
Long Distance Information in *UTS Review*
Amaze Your Friends in *Famous Reporter* & *Tin Fish*
American Friends in on-line magazines *Slope* and *Big Bridge*
Traffic Noises in *Sidewalk.*
Tiepolo appeared in *Shampoo* and as a limited edition book
designed and printed by Brendan O'Brien
Roman Friends appeared in *Let's Get Lost* with poems by Pam Brown & Laurie Duggan
both of whom I thank for reading many of the poems in this book

Contents

Flash and Baci

Three Poems For John Forbes

Newer Poems

The Misfits

Flash and Baci

Home Town

Driving into work while
Cath reads about driving around London
& wondering when will I next write a poem
or whether to just work on *Gwendolyn*
a poem of John's & mine & maybe I should
it *is* half mine, I drop Cath off, do a
U-turn & scoot down to the EAF, park, go inside
check the mail empty my bag a little
lock up again & set off for the coffee shop
where I'll read or write a poem or a
review—or work on *Gwendolyn*, I suppose, is
a possibility ... I feel sophisticated to be
wearing my long black coat—which, however,
does not really make me look
like my idea of a New Yorker: it's a little
beaten & more groovy than suave
& doesn't reflect wealth, & the thought of
my poverty—when I ask for coffee—makes
me amused & reflective. "The heater's on,"
I say to the waitress. And she says "Yes.
You like?" "It's Great!" I say. It is.
I ask could I have some banana cake please
with such diffidence she is surprised and
I realize the thoughts about my poverty
& entitlements have affected my emotions a little.
She says I *can* have some & goes off to get it.

Which is where the poem could end. It could all
be about the small things in life—how I

do get coffee etc.
Cath thought Laurie's
latest poem could be broken up into lots of
smaller ones, or broken with numbers, asterisks—
so you'd know when to stop re-read & have a think (etcetera).
Not that she wanted little poems, of shape & mild
flick-of-the-wrist closure.
This waitress has served me coffee
for over ten years now. She used to work at the *Flash Café*
—actually called *Flash Gelateria*—but known to most as just
'*The Flash*'—but they changed hands finally
& she came down here where this new place opened. Whose name
I don't even know—where I've been coming nearly a year
now. What *is* it called? *Baci*—I look out the window
find the sign. *The Baci* is big & airy—you can stay all day
I imagine. The view is very Richard Estes—in a busy kind of way—
which *I* think recommends it. Though to whom does it
recommend it? No one I know, to speak to, daily
knows Richard Estes' paintings. Except Paul, & Richard
at a guess—Richard would & Paul would like the aesthetic
though not, probably, the art—my only Ruscha friend,
Paul—"if I may so term his aesthetic". (Ha Ha.)
Though who am I on daily speaking terms with? Cath
—& Laurie & Pam & John Forbes & John Jenkins—
in my mind. Realler I guess than talking to Frank O'Hara
or Tony Towle—whose speaking voice I have no idea of—
probably silent &, alternatively, garrulous. I imagine him
mostly staring plumply out a picture window—floor to ceiling
—is that 'picture'?—hands in pockets, shirt untucked slightly
saying something rhapsodic & complaining. It's dark outside
& raining. Hullo, Tony. There, I did it. Now I realize
I am beginning to talk like him. Which amuses me—though

talking like him is not my purpose. What *is* my purpose in life?
the joke answer & the serious, & why am I not up to either
or both? Because that's life. One is to fail exemplarily.
"We are gathered here today ladies & gentlements . . ."—SPLASH—
Somebody has fallen off the pier. The Fellini figure pauses briefly
& they carry on—it was Malcolm Lowry, the outsider. He
fell off. Not me—I'm in the Richard Estes painting
in the middle of Adelaide, that only I know about,
going, tonight, to the Post-West opening, that everybody
knows about. Their shows are so frequent & the gallery
so small I think the artists have them just to drink
& natter every fortnight. Though tonight the art
promises to be good, or not hurtful, maybe in fact allright.

*

When I get there Richard is sitting against the wall with Suzie.
Paul is hanging about the door, drink in hand. He does
know Richard Estes I am relieved to find out
& I talk to all the artists—Aldo & Shaun, & Louise
shows up & later Michael & Mary. Shaun's bought my book.
We discuss Raymond Roussel, Micky Allan's photographs,
Harry Mathews, Perec, Svevo, Jr Walker & Wilson Pickett,
employment

*

What matters?   What is important
to say?
                    From reading all morning
I can manage
                    a series of assertions

—or I feel that way—
I can remember
none, right now
except: "Daniel Buren's art—
(followed by some blunt denial of his importance)"
But I always knew that.

Walking into town
to deliver an article to the
Advertiser
feeling deliciously alone
—& modern,
the way John Tranter feels
when he cleans the pool,
but actually for the Tranter/Benjamin reason
: Paris,
the streets, arcades, the
winter light & clouds, the
suggestion of rain
another article done, anonymous,
but it will appear above my name
but I feel anonymous—
I see Tubby Justice across the street, waiting.
I wave.
She waves, & disappears
hurries off, ahead. I smile
& she reappears & we say hullo. My friends
are like ghosts in Adelaide.
What is real here? The only
intelligent people I know who read the *Advertiser*
buy it for the TV guide & movies
& I think movies

are crap.
That's about it
for my relation to an
audience.
Still, it helped me feel modern
that day
crossing the road. I could just
as easily
have written a poem—
& I'd've felt okay
in that light, in that atmosphere, in that coat,
in that cold, amongst the early morning crowd, in
the Central Business District
though strangely, I'd've felt less a
public person—more crestfallen
as Tubby disappeared,
scarcely assuaged when she reappeared
can "assuaged"
float about free like that?
can only hurt be
assuaged? or something analogous?
Adelaide
looked so Kertész at that moment
Life could make you
weep
It would given time, but we move so quickly—
it
will, in time, maybe. Time now
to look for John Forbes
to read
to calm down : I can't find my *Strange
Days Ahead* (Michael Brownstein) a much liked book

to check from the cover how to spell Kertész
& get it right
I am mad—but it must be somewhere
I sometimes imagine
an open letter to Peter Schjeldahl
but there is so much I admire
that he doesn't like
(e.g., Brownstein)
though I admire *him*—
would that be a basis on which to write?
So much of what
I write is an open letter to someone : Laurie, Pam
or is meant
to be read aloud by my collected peers a small society
that doesn't exist, unfortunately, around a table
like
the Royal Society
meeting somewhere
—instead, like Tubby,
they go their own way
each isolated, with their own projects,
own worries, own apostrophized thoughts / complaints to / versions
of things
as do I.
It is not Kertész anyway
on Brownstein's book. It's Sander. I *did* mean Kertész. On the streets
of Adelaide does anyone resemble the portraits of Sander? Some. But
who stands still that long? Not me.
Here
are the newer John Forbes poems, in the later pages
looking
for a good first line :

here's one with Spencer Tracy—
though I see it says "Spent tracer
flecks Baghdad's sky"
—I'm going blind—
& there's the one for me "Frank O'Hara
never went skating
but he liked to dance."
If O'Hara
taught us timing like the poem says,
I wish I'd paid attention.
Did I learn anything from him?
it has worn off with this moving around.

Walk on the Wild Side

Tomorrow: shop, bank, wash hair.
Gym
        fix salad
                maybe put prices
on the new books arrived at
the E.A.F.
            I guess read the paper
                            have
coffee. An eventful day? There
are new poems to work on at last
—I left these at the E.A.F., tonight—
there are poems of Miriel's to look over,
dinner at Cath's.
                Anyway,
                        now
I take Little Walter off
                    and put on
Lou Reed—*Walk on the Wild Side*—
not a judgement :
                I will put
Little Walter on
                a lot more times
in my life.
                Lou is sweet
. . . and I read the poems of James
Schuyler, the one about Auden, the one
about
        Dining Out with Doug and Frank.
Better than sweet.

I mean, I *love* Lou—
but this is something else.
—Time goes by.
I put the record back to the first track.—
Actually, Lou *reads* some of these guys.
I wonder if he reads Jimmy Schuyler.
Or does he only read
the Burroughs / Warhol
connection?
Probably not. But *probably*
he had some one-liner
summation
of the
New York 'School'—
that let him off
the hook.
I wouldn't
have him
be different.
—Time passes.—
Well,
a great poet!
I listen
to *Walk on the*
Wild Side again.
Sleep.

Poem

—for Martin Munz

Walking down from the *Star*
Grocery from the far side
of Morphett Street I saw

the lion on top of the Lion Building
The first time I have
noticed it, in quite a while.

Its scale is increasingly
and loveably inappropriate
to North Terrace, as it modernizes

and the lion seems small
earnest, and straightforward.
And the sky looks great beyond it.

I have chocolate frogs
for Becky and Julie
—for Martin I just

casually stroll into the Park Lane
Liquor Store
and order a bottle of Strega

—no, Martin is in Sydney . . .

and that is a joke . . .
a famous poem
by a favourite poet

has something like that sequence—
gifts bought for people and the stroll
for the Strega purchase. My life

is miles from that—I wear
a battered leather jacket that
if I thought about I'd be embarrassed

—when could *I*
last afford scotch for someone,
or go to a dinner laden with presents?

on the other hand—I *am* a poet.

Different stars shine down on me. I am on

the other side of the world.

Today I talked to Yvonne Rainer,
a New York artist. I said, Hullo,
I liked your film. And then I asked her

about the dedication to Ronald Bladen
—"in memoriam"—I didn't know
that he was dead. She asked—

and I said I knew just the few
well known works
and had for years. She said

he was a painter originally, romantic,
expressionist.
There was going to be a retrospective.

I held Bladen's work in only
an affectionate regard. I think I had
originally thought not much of it

—but the most usual photo of one,
The Big X (his sculpture) I had liked
and had liked to do drawings of,

sending it up, but liking it really.

At the far end of the photo
beyond the enormous X that filled
the two storey gallery, which had

classical pillars around it,
was a 19th century Roman sculpture—
Diana, say—some modest naked

nymph or woman, such a
strange contrast to the big minimal
sculpture. I used to like doing the

drawing, to bring out this contrast.
Once I put also two people in it
small, obviously walking and talking,

oblivious, to the sculpture and the statue.
Did I? or were they
always in the photo?

I write my first fan letter—
to a favourite poet in America. I had
intended to for years. I had intended to write

to others:
Joe Turner . . .
This week

I have been confused, and
acting strangely, my heart
in panic at its foolishness.

This—
is a day for decisions. I orientate myself
between a Frank O'Hara poem and the sculpture,

and this new information
about Ronald Bladen, and the little lion
on the "Lion" *building*

—in my leather jacket,
that looks, now that I recall it, like one
James Schuyler wears

in an early photograph
and that looks very 'unlike'
him

—the bomber jacket
—on such a poet—as unlikely as it
looks on me—but then, I am

hardly *here* I guess. I
know the lion is doomed, more or less,
but I will likely be gone before it. Is that

true? Well, the *thought* is to the point.
It is the Canutish aspect to the lion I love—
standing dark and silhouetted,

against the brilliant clouded sunsets—
that seem like history

Halogen Pam

I picture
Pam's halogen lamp sending
a warm cone of light down

onto her desk
—white—
& the warm, transparent brown brandy

—or what was the drink?—sits there—

—still,
exuding calm
& "just reward"

—merely by its light translucence—

undisturbed.
Pam is seated to right, a silhouette
down lower than the desk, somehow, as I picture it—
reading;

determinedly—& successfully—'lost'—
after the irritation of walking home from work
into a drying, hair-blowing wind.

But she is fractiously lost, at best, her mind
coming back to sorrows, till the book succeeds—
in calming her to think them through,

or to leave them & follow the book, talk to Jane,
check the garden or whatever it is that
Pam does do—shower, change her clothes,

do some washing & read again then hang the washing
out & cook maybe & plan the night: to
read or write or watch television,

or go out: I think she & Jane
visit more—than I do. Though I expect
visits would be planned, arranged more in advance

& she would likely not have had the drink or done the chores
or would have done them at once if they were going out.
The idea of the casual visit—of dropping in—of even
        ringing,

to say *"I'm coming over—alright?"*
is a dream it seems, for me, though why is that?
I know no one, have no transport, never 'think'

to use the phone (have work, am tired . . .)—habits,
developed over time, to keep me from what I might do.
What kind of friend can I be—to my friends—really?

A disappointment. Imagining the drink,
standing, still, in a deep, 'martini' glass,
I try to imagine it as painted: but I imagine it more 'real'

than Vuillard, who would be intimate enough—more
detailed, less modish, than Margaret Preston, not
as brushy as a Monet flower piece—a still-life I saw in

a catalogue recently that was so evenly
& thickly inflected—all grey? all rose? like a Leon Kossoff—
is that right?—but far nicer: every stroke was

small & flicked & petal-shaped—pink (or grey) &
loaded with white & it was an instant of perception
of contentment heightened & raised & made live on—

but when I return to what I'm thinking about—the picture
    of Pam—
it is inappropriate. I think briefly of Janet Fish (it
should be more clean-lined) whom I had not thought about much,

in years, though I have not forgotten—a picture
I saw of hers once made an impression though I am not sure
at this distance how great or how reasonable

that impression was. It was a picture of gin bottles—
up close—Gordons or Gilbeys—through which
light reflected & bounced. A kind of new realism—a

bit like early Susan Norrie—though less claustrophobic, less
boringly pointed—though in the book I saw the Janet Fish in,
the reason why I think of her again—it is surrounded

by other artists doing similar things to Norrie. (So that
    kind of thing
happened in America, too: overdetermined: the time required it
though it didn't need it (much) (if you ask *my* opinion—

anyway, I'm giving it). Walter Sickert, maybe, could paint it,
though I want less gloom. Anyway—I was going to say—
Richard made this joke about Janet Fish when I pointed to it

how she was like [someone he named] only obviously on
    hallucinogens
& alcoholic. It sounded pretty funny. Only,
I didn't get the art reference & so I don't remember it.

It would be great to visit Pam now—
for a few stiff drinks—just ghost in &
sit, or stand—having them with her,

looking out the window

at the garden, or the harbour, modern,
neither at a restaurant, which is too noisy & 'ends' anyway,
or at a loss for words (because I'm no conversationalist)

& ghost out again, conversation done, or just
sink to the floor drunk mildly (though thoroughly),
a visitation.

*

as I sit in this coffee shop Pam,
the next morning, about to send this letter, to you,
& this poem—looking out

at the Richard Estes view—maybe
from this angle it is Ralph Goings—
I watch some twenty year old drunks

carousing a little as they cross the street
pathetically buoyed by their idea of themselves—
drunk still, at 10 in the morning,

pretending to hail a car, in whose way
they nearly get in crossing
& stagger down the road less heroic than they imagine

in pale t-shirts & baggy shorts & thongs, gormless.

I have behaved that way too, in all probability
though less through certainty in my uniform
or my enlistment in the order of good ol boys.

But certain about something, probably.
Best not to think about it. Conformism does
make people feel better: *I* like being a human too—

& the differences I congratulate myself on
don't measure up to much.

                                        You probably do remember
Richard Estes, Pam. Typically he paints
a photographic looking New Realism: a line of

new pickup trucks, parked out the back,
of *The Texas* 'Bean' *Diner*—all shiny & bleakly
meaningless—plenty of blue sky, lots of

chrome & glass & metallic paint-job & cement & macadam.

Reality looks better, though sometimes it is
aided by resembling these pictures.

Pam, you've tried
Adelaide—& it didn't work for you. Otherwise
you could be here. Would we see each other much
living in the same city?

Sydney—could I live there & be happy?

After all, you can't spend all your time
looking at the harbour, listening to the frangipani leaves
slither & rattle, late at night, a drink in your hand

feeling cheerfully or mellowly existential. After all, do *you*?

Though there are other things to Sydney—the balmy,
milky, soft air on a cool summer day,
the radios buzzing with the races, that emanate quietly
from the pubs &

TABs, the old men in thongs, cigarettes in their
t-shirt sleeves,
so nicely seedy, the corner shops—but these things
are tiny patches:
of Annandale, & other bits—of 100 yards or less—of

footpath and aged picket fence, & the mixture of cars—
broken &
flash—the particular charm of which
is tolerance for everything else, or reads that way.

One facet of a tough city. Can you 'say' that?
And there's the poetry scene.
(One down here too.)

"Decoupage"—I guess that does mean putting
a lining inside something (a box you said) rather than
cutting little bits, from the top of a box, to make it

castellated—like a toy soldiers' fort—because you say
        you are doing it
to some cupboards too. I have an image of you & Jane,
in triangular paper hats, dressed in primary colours

holding aloft small wooden half-swords,

bursting out of open cupboards (slightly castellated)
—a crowded, vertical composition—a little like
those de Chirico gladiators: *they're* usually

waving their swords about—with a bit of pillar handy
& one incongruous lounge chair,
a fallen bit of pediment—though my picture of you & Jane

is more 'Stanley Spencer'—though less crowded
& manic & airless. Though anyone who *behaved* like that—
imagine stepping into your house & finding you & Jane yelling
        & whooping

looking up, interrupted, while playing 'pirates'!
At that thought I nearly spit nonexistent cake
        from my mouth
—a noise like a motorbike starting—the little Greek man opposite

looks up. We often sit at tables near each other—he
with *The Greek Herald*, me with *The Guardian*. (Didn't you know
I was English?)

Actually, Pam, you *should move* down here: I go outside—
& the air is exactly what I want from Sydney—so moist
it is almost cool, & softly bright—& there's another thing

that is very Sydney—or Melbourne's idea of Sydney—the great
doorway to the T-shirt shop, filled with the fake jaws of a shark—
that you step through. When it first opened up

I saw a Japanese tourist
delightedly getting his wife to photograph him
standing in it. Unfortunately, the t-shirts they sell

are terrible—full of jokes about sharks—gross
views of Australian life, the sense of humour they appeal to
making one despair—of creeping Americanization
—like an old man.

On the other hand, they seem to be going out of business.

I write this
with a pencil—it's my lunchbreak now (these last
seven lines). But the pencil drags too slow—

on this particular paper—so I stop here:
back at the same table
in the coffee shop.

I read instead.

Poem (Dynamic Sleeper)

Cath
—a dynamic sleeper—
makes a curved nougat line
under the doona, an
islamic-looking comma,
her dark head at the end.

As I try to figure
what *I* am
Cath has moved

(I sit beside)

(& think of Laurie & Pam
why is it always them? &
when I think that I think: Dennis, John Forbes—
& Johnny J.
Anna Couani

Mary Christie
Bronwyn Platten
Mill.
Becky Davis
—a warrior tomorrow.

Thom Corcoran—

Thinking: maybe I will write
a little like Mr Whalen

Shoot off a few opinions
All isolated from each other

Tho he is a Buddhist &
          the ideas
      hang together

          —I am
just some
                    divided nutter

Is man not naturally good, Mr Johnson?
No Madam, no more than a wolf!
And woman? No more so. This is worse than Swift (sotto voce
says woman)

Scenes of Life at the Capital
     (I am reading)

Margot is going to curate some Adelaide
Postmodern   for the regional galleries
almost ten years post time

At the Flash I read the paper

At the Baci I think & stare

& write review of Anton.
& finish it home in bed.

a good idea I nearly have
goes wandering—to where in
the room?
I sit patiently
for its return   A couple of times it
nearly comes   goes off again
it is a good thought—I know—at
last it comes   I write it down

Emm.

Yesterday I was offered
8 "contact hours"—teaching—
at the art school—no preparation
Maybe they *want* me
to just shoot off
random ideas—
free associate
from my 'collected' 'wisdom'
(groan)

the knowledge I have
gained
in all my years of careful
—carefree?—
unemployment

underqualified

finally, not having done 'anything'
has come to seem
the ultimate wisdom?

Is it the reviewing : he has opinions—
he can teach our students ! (?)

Honours course on Popular Culture !
(hilarious)

To tune of *"Yesterday"* intones:
Underdale
do-doot do do do do *doot* do-do

I remember when we (every week) drove through Thirroul
I would sing Thigh *rule* thigh*ruuule . . . it's*
a wonderful place
to tune of
NY NY

Probably an endlessly talking David Antin / is /
"what this place needs"

Well I'm not it

most art ideas are so easy to poke your
finger thru   you have
to watch your 'lip'   (self
censorship)

most art fails as art : most craft succeeds as craft (Maxim)

but that's its trip! that's
why we like it, or are interested

This is not the materialist or sociological view
—tho I can talk that way, too—

but why not? at the bottom of the pyramid
is art school—*most* of the students don't become
artists—perfectly consonant with that
/ is / most artists don't hit the target
we admire it cause it's difficult—
or rare

imagine talking the other jargon : common sense,
deconstruction, & cultural studies
"The Cultural Efficacy of *Hey Dad*"

I see Becky at work over the weekend : they won
the game (hockey) against
a team of toughies. She was
looking forward to it,
a toughie herself

And now—months later (I'm
in bed again, writing this—
she is leaving : 4 years
in the job—the best person—
why didn't I get to know her?

better ? more ?
I don't want her to go—
why can't she stay?   She can't
that's all
—moving on;
moving away

I remember when she first came:
"weren't but 'this' high"

"Scenes of Life at the Capital"

now I am at the capital—Sydney—
attending to the last years
of my dad
closing up the house
putting him on a plane, an emotional
time
When he's on the plane
I will phone Pam—till now
I have been so taken up with my father
cooking talking finalising accounts
care of the house the redirecting of mail
I have not been able to call /
anyone—
not with a view to meeting.

I'm glad I did : it's been an
intense time.

I am in bed again—that will be the
principle of the poem maybe—
"Poem written in bed"

in beds.

Is *that* the kind of poet
he is?—makes me sound
like Rochester, John Wilmot
a 17th century rake

alternatively, someone who almost
never sleeps : 3 times to bed in
so many months (!)

To Generalize

We sit at a table in *The Baci*,
an indoor table—
with a view of the tables outside, that may act
as a springboard,
the false limb,
or 'pseudopod',
of a primitive one-cell animal,
which
—tho to
what end—
I compare our brains to:

We are *not* outdoors, no
But we are not quite *inside*
either

—because of the windows—
Tho should it rain
we are entirely inside, & glad
of it.
(In fact, it *won't* rain.
And—
another fact—the fan is on 'too hard'

—but half an hour, what *is*
a lunch hour, that one can afford
to move,
or complain,

unless one does it *right away*?

Yep?

Right?)

Take *The Guardian*, a newspaper :
open it—& you are transported,
far away.
I sit, 'literally', in *The Baci*, the
literal one—others sit, or sit metaphorically,
as you do, Reader,
at metaphorical *Bacis* & think away too, aware,
as I am—*for I 'generalize'*—
of the larger world, the larger tides

& patterns that
pass through it,

& of their smallness
& the incidental nature

of their own lives
in relation *to* these tides,

even of the
invigoratingly

'human dimension'
this knowledge lends

—& its practical inutility.
You look outside, at the beautiful, slightly glaring light
that lands on *Cacas' Chemists*—& lands, too,
on whatever *you're* looking at—& consider the traffic,
the passersby,
the scope of the disasters in Africa—which is almost
Medieval—though modern because man-made—
& the scandals in the City—which are Hogarthian,
English, & 18th century, though modern, too—
& your *own* problems, which are contingent &
practical—how to rob a bank,
(whether to move from that fan) whether
to get another coffee—which you *need*
if it is metaphorical & this stuff
brings you down.

If it is *not* metaphorical
but a real one, you must have
a whole hour for your lunch hour—
mine has 30 minutes.

2

Now, did you take your newspaper? No?
Take mine, the *Guardian.* It is an eye,
a balloon on which you float, "Eighty Days" style,
around the world, never really touching down,
and also, of course, like a limb. You pick it up,
hit something with it,
perhaps a fly. And the world
is that li'l bit littler.
Or it is a steady state.
There are people bashing flies

all over the world—*Hong Kong Herald* here,
Bombay Tribune there, *The Lima Truth*, Montreal's
famous *Examiner*—killing perhaps the only fly
in that part of Canada—or did it get away. Who knows? The
waitress looks up—
what is that guy
swatting at,
at **The '*Syrup & Muffin*' Diner**? He settles down.
Her eyes
return to the jars in front of her.

Your eye
takes in the window
& the scene outside—cars, pedestrians, *Cacas the Chemist*—
& is 'drawn' outside, & with it you
(with the assent of your brain—which in truth
according to some theories, is
an outgrowth, a sophistication, a *development*
of that optical organ) are drawn outside also.
You arrive together, your eye delighted,
your brain keeping up, & your 'self' rounding out their number,
invigorating to be up & doing—up &
'going', unfortunately, back to work—
in five more minutes.

A Picture

In Manet's great painting
The Insomniacs the three readers

share the bed and white
bedspread, two with books held up before them

reading, a girl and her mother,
the other, a man, has books too, on the bedspread before him

but writes in a pad—*in* pencil *on* a pad—
their story. His books are:

(black and white)—the poems of Towle—
and (pink and black)—Violi.

The girl, who lies on her back, and holds her book—
a pumpkin yellow, with blue and red flashes in it—almost above her,

reads *Mallory and the Mystery Diary*. Her mother, beside her,
and who reads propped up—

though she has slid down a little
by the time

of the moment the picture is showing—

has a pile of books,
between herself and the girl—where their knees would be. These

are chiefly blue, and the book
she holds is green and black, *Troubled Waters*.

You can see
that the woman's face

is of a type much used
by the Impressionists, by Manet and Morisot, the features

delicate and a little sharp, rather than round.
But it is not Morisot's face

as painted by Manet, or
as in Morisot's

portrait of herself—or Monet's
last portrait, of his wife, as she lay dying—

though it has that *imprecision*, which makes it seem
'Vuillardy'—

it is Cath Kenneally,
wearing a round-necked top

of the palest, scrambled-egg
yellow, thinking deeply—

yet attuned—at least slightly—to the girl,
her daughter, beside her, wearing lilac pyjamas.

Anna. Her face
is round, unlike her mother's, and her eyes are wide and dark—

where her mother's
are paler, green—and her hair

is long, and braided in one
single plait—pulled behind, *in-*

visible in the painting, which emphasizes (or only sees)
the subsequently rounded head. Her

mother's hair, by contrast,
is dark and a little red—and short and stylistically

a jarring note in Manet's painting—or might
perhaps be

if the painting's manner were sufficiently sharp,
detailed enough, to pick this up—but the brushwork

is very generalized and summary: who would notice?

Beside them I am more incongruous.
I have a watch on for one thing

though in the style I am proposing it could read as
anything (a bracelet?)—a smear of colour

at the wrist, the kind of detail that remains inexplicable—
but incidental even in a style this broad

and part of what . . . well, what Manet saw—
and which makes it all convincing, as a gestalt. (A word

I guess Manet did not use: they talked though
of the decorative effect, the unity, and truth and sincerity—

"Nature through a temperament.") The watch hand
goes to my head

which is bent, writing, writing this.
I tell the girls, and we all look up: Anna smiles,

Cath looks 'poised' and I, because I've been concentrating,
have a frown disappearing. Hi.

Mostly Hindley Street

"He never spoke out"—Mathew Arnold

I think the same thing is happening again

Same waitress same coffee same
street
"A black coffee & a . . .
. . . Baclava."
"We're out, I'm sorry."
"Oh well,"
—points to rumbaba—
"The rumbaba."

I take it to my table
A big smile
to the waitress
who has brought me coffee
for 15 years now
less some years
than others
& look at the view
the State
Bank
or some bank
its name changing
as it goes broke, gets bailed out, gets
sold off
same building at any rate
floating there, handsome, in the grey rainy
sky

above the small-town, 1930s, two-storey
street facades
on Hindley Street
housing
pleasantly cruddy, & crass, dance clubs, drink
barns, & . . . *Hellenic Travel* . . . *The Singing Restaurant!*
one I never noticed
must've opened in the last
week or so, or is it still being renovated
for its
dismal tuneful future?
dismal & short I imagine
& tune*less*

If I feel happy again

isn't that *good*?

The radio's playing *Werewolf Of London*

how nice of them
& I exit & stomp
confidently to work
Ar—ooo!

Well, I *will*.
For now, I look
out the window at all the clean surfaces—lovely
New Realism-style colours.
A terrible
art movement—

                                        paintings mostly dull—
but it sure made reality look good for
looking a bit like it—as if the art movement
gave a certain style of scene
                                                            an ideal
                                                                        to live up to
—to which,
            in certain conditions—
                                                              bit of ‘down & out’, bit
of nothing-going-on
                                                &
                                                              the right light—
it could aspire
                                          Suck in that gut! straighten
that back!
                                        pull the collar up &
forward slightly,
                                                    act casual!
                                                                          & my heart goes out.

I write to Laurie
                                        about Thomas Gray, & his
short walks
                                        a man well before his time—

he’d’ve loved   day time TV

                                                              Anyway, taking a
short walk now
                                        I see Millie’s friend Steve

lead singer with *Free Moving Curtis*

a band

named after a black male Barbie Doll

that

never sold in Australia: I think they saw an ad for it
in a magazine & loved the name

Steve

was something of a martyr to day time TV himself
when he lived at Westbury Street, as I remember

I could come out at almost any time & there he'd
be

watching it   late at night   early in the morning

day time TV   he watched the worst of whatever was on:

Late at night he could find Day Time TV

tho

—unlike Thomas Gray—

(!)

Steve was steeling
himself, pondering, planning his future

I see him
now making long strides down Hindley
past *Cacas Chemist's*, past *Jerusalem Sheshkebab*,
& on

tight black jeans, his hair reddish for
a change—

pursuing the gig I guess

"He never spoke out."

Unlike Thomas Gray Steve speaks out

regularly

a band of humour

& rage

At least, I *hear* they're okay.

Gray wrote that *one* poem, more or less, &
seven others

—nothing for years on end—

saying 'it pays to keep busy'

so he catalogued this, made

a list of that, wrote in the margins of his books—
taught nothing, wrote nothing, "he never spoke out,"
Arnold said

—& went for short walks, as I told

Laurie, collected seeds, grew some flowers in his rooms. He
"kept himself *to* himself"—a phrase
I always loved—Yes, he did that, too.

Of course

it is a short walk

to the EAF

(where I will walk)

Will Steve

hit the big time?

the odds are against it
More chance in poetry (!)

—tho a smaller

big time

I bought some chive seeds myself

last week
That I probably won't even get round
to planting
—tho Cath will.

I see I am
drawing
a comparison
& that it can't make me
very happy.

The fortunes of a lunch hour—

one moment exhilarated

moments later—gloom

I guess these are the rocky rapids, & breakers,
Gray rode at the refectory
imagined slights
of the undergraduates of Cambridge

Prithee, what
does Mr Gray 'do'?
<u>Nothing</u>.

Well, I hear he *'Never Speaks Out'*!   (huh-ha-hah)

Letter from Laurie today
who says
Wasn't Gray supposed to be a "bit of a prig"?

Well—
the impression he gave

& tho the biography hates Arnold's
phrase

& attempts to defend Gray's life on the graveyard
shift
staying 'occupied'   collecting buds
noting the
weather
the arrival of the first grasshoppers
& emendations to various lexicons

—his *fear* of giving his
first lecture :
& which he never gave—

still, . . .

Yes
"prig" came to mind—
along with "insipid"

all to an almost hilarious degree applicable

& the 'life'   of quietism & depression—maybe
(the only excuse)   he couldn't help it.

One can
imagine

Samuel Johnson headbutting him

"Gray was dull sir.

Dull in public, dull in his closet, dull to himself.
He invented a new way of being dull—
and some people admired him for it."

They never

met.

Gray saw him in the street once, lumbering
past, & said—"There goes Ursa Major."

Prig &

Drip

of the first order.

*

Tonight I talk on Modernism—

(Rock Hudson

leans to Doris Day's ear

"The arts shall march

in the very van . . ."

"Oh, Rock! Cut it out!")

—but tonight I do—*post* modernism, too!

*

Very full today, *The Baci*

Which I remark

to the waitress

who looks almost relieved
when I say it

Mill!

who I will ring
when I get to Brisbane in a few weeks time.

Not John Stuart Mill
—Millie Dickins.

Sitting here in the pub

Feeling like *Whistler's Mother*—

Waiting for Crab

This always happens
tho tonight I don't mind
(yet)

(in another *hour* I'll be
dis-satisfied)
in black jeans,
black-brown ('coal'?) jumper

—Yves Saint-Laurent ?
someone French—

long black coat

In the corner seat
in the quiet 'nook'

writing
drinkin', thinkin', writin', sittin'

a smile to this couple here
that guy there
her
A bit of a look
at the Brute who approaches
the bar
(large guy, officer, of the 'Brute' type—
enormous jaw, flat nose—seems
,actually, Mr Gentle

I rock back & forth

like Whister's mother, like *Crabby*'s mom
many times since,
thinking
When will he come?
Where *is* that boy?
Actually I look a
little more like,
probably,
the companion to that painting, a
symphony in grey,
the portrait of Carlysle—
or was it Ruskin?—
some prim dork sitting stiffly

a little huffily in a chair in his greatcoat—

as I sit here. *When in walks Crab . . . !*

The fat guy, outside
the tattoo shop,
holds a baby on his
chest—well, sitting on
the swell of his big black T-shirt.
A wife—girlfriend, sister,
defacto sister-in-law—watches.
A *paterfamilias* act
on-the-cheap.
                    (We
don't like each other, it is
true: he felt some need
to crowd me on the footpath one night,
to assert what he imagines
is superiority.   Oh well,
who's perfect? Not me.
                    Not him.)

                                        Has
my coffee shop shed custom—
in the change to smaller premises?
I want it to survive.

A little 'man'—that is, a kid

probably—cycles by. No hands.
A courier, seemingly rolling up
the cuffs of his gloves—looking remarkably like
the bad guy in *Doonesbury*. (Duke?
is that his name? the one with
the Vietnamese girl assistant?
who does scams?) Same large head,
same nose—& crash helmet &
goggles making the face look large
& caricatured.

This takes
longer to describe than his
whipping past!

No Futurist I!—

just a moseyin' kind of guy.
(Hi, pard.)

Anyway, now he's gone—in fact
he appeared only briefly in the space
between a car & a truck—

("I did but see him
passing by—& thought
Doonesbury")

& I look at my short black
take a last taste
& return to work

I write a bit more
of the Richard Grayson review
add a word
I'd been waiting to appear in my memory
—since I started it
some days ago—
Simone
rang just before I left for lunch
from
another gallery
to ask
Did the E.A.F.
have a hot glue gun?
Nuh
was the answer, finally—
when I had looked around—
I wished her luck

her show 'opens' tonight.

Things, in art,
are always very last minute.
or, like Michael's piece
(last minute, too?)
they don't work
the day *after* the opening.
So *I* ring *them*.
("Your show isn't working.")

I forgot to bring the Tranter interview
—about
how he's *tired* of poetry

—Well, who isn't?
tho when you're writing it
you wouldn't do anything else.

What I *will* do
'tho'
is go back to work—in
just 10 minutes.
Dinner, tonight, with Cath
whom I always have dinner with
but dinner 'out'
is our plan
& afterwards, Crab
—Crab's band—
plays at the Exeter
& we might brave the
beergarden—enclosed
but, in winter, still cold—
the cigarette smoke
& all the rest, to hear them
drummer, trombone & a sax
sort of *Salvos-*
do-Fred Wesley
—and—*Swordfishtrombone*,
only piquant.
We'll see.

News of the Day

je est un autre—Arthur Rimbaud
I'se another, too!—Lou Costello

Peter B.   poet in Rome
w. "difficult second album" problems
—follow-up to first book, need
to be different etc

I spend the morning
giving (an) improvised talk
to high school students

on *The Nature*
of the E.A.F.
& *intro*   to a rather formalist, light,
&
decorative   artist
Naturally emphasising his
'conceptual' bits

My own difficult   xth book
—difficult "whatever" book—
will be coming out soon,
one in which
I emphasize "the conceptual
bits", too

(Unshaven

& slightly boho looking:

I hope this
contradicts

interestingly

the 'aesthete' piece of my
talk

tho the students
as likely
—as correctly, too—
thought
What a dill.)

I don't
'know'

that my poems
say anything new

'conceptually'

well maybe they do

—Doomed to say

everything
twice—
(Twice! you should
be so lucky. Twice!)

Don't the Velvet Underground do?
(say things twice) ?
[& I quote]
"too-too, too much"

I ain't
never had
Too Much Fun !

((wistfully))

A blues I sing, one way
or another
in every poem

: I've

had
'enough'.
I've
had a little—
but I ain't never had . . .   (etc)

#

This place
. . . the students here . . .
Uni students this time
—mostly Japanese, all
talking to each other: it is
pleasantly
animated: every
word
emphasised easily

as they
read essay questions
out
quizzically

quotes from articles
etc
their beautiful voices
sophisticated

Optimistic

about their futures

Actually, I look around
& she is
Indian
Tho the ones in view
(male & female,
in pairs,   at every
table)

are Asian.

(Business Studies)

Then,

some mixed—

foreign & Australian.

Some all-Australian tables

me

all Australian—

you Jane?

*

(Sweet Jane.

*

<u>*doo*</u>-do <u>*doo*</u>-do,

<u>*doot*</u> doo . . .)

*

Anyone who had a brain

you think that
they would use it

Not me
I’m going back to ***work*** in just a second!

(in
a ‘sec’!)

*

An essay
By a poet I
. . . well, *‘like’*, but regard
As something of an

apostate

Saying what I think

but wish she hadn’t said

—So *that’s* the Church I’m in!—

Explains

that it is not a

matter
of explaining yourself

I buy a pen from the Chinese lady

in the Chinese
shop
pale mauve
(She offered me black)

(Out of deference to my
Baudelairean demeanour)

*

Kids seem to have invaded the city again
—is it
holiday time?—
the girls being cute, the guys being
tough
ho hum
How much
longer will I inhabit
etcetera

*

Howard looks more glumly simian
than ever

chump, chimp, & PM

Sumo wrestlers, soon, come to
town
The Japanese student who lives with us
—Tomoko—
briefly interested

Nostalgia for home
where uncle and brother
are enthusiasts
where the domestic
noise
of them,

watching it on television . . .
so much more familiar than the sound
here—
where, however, Tomoko *fits in*

Foreigners, us.

I'm
just an other myself
a line I think I have
never read in the

original

imagine having only read the original

Julia Kristeva's little head
looks at me quizzically

from the book on the table
near where my coffee once was

—swept now to the kitchen

by the cook
a cheerful type,   in high spirits:
I think
it is his first day—

her head rests on her hand

(&)   in the light of what I've said
is
severe
disapproving.

"Ideas come to us as the successors to griefs."

Remember how world weary we would feel
adult, woozily melancholic,

iron entering the soul
at 15 ?
when the Walker Brothers sang
"The Sun Ain't Gonna Shine Anymore" ?
They sing it now
on the coffeeshop radio

altering the whole *key*
of my thought

I exit —at last, & briefly—
"considered"

A noble teenage
sentiment
wrapped about me

which I never thought would
still fit

manfully I stride

thoughtless, modern

mildly sad a little blank unaggrieved

to the
traffic light
where I think, *straight against the light I cross*

but wait

Giles Auty Furioso

"We have noticed a marked decline in deference."
—*The Spectator*, 1997

"I think continually of those who were truly great,"
someone said, but I like to think of things like
the *erased de Kooning*, as considered by, say, Giles Auty.

I'm funny that way.
I'm funny like that.
That way I'm funny.
(Etc.)
—Sol Le Witt

I used to find amusing the idea of
Donald Brook greeting Cy Twombly—
like King George. *Scribble, scribble, scribble,*
eh Mr Twombly.
But, as the artist's funny name
has grown more prominent the anecdote
about Gibbon & George
has been forgotten.
I can't *do* that
any more

Without entering the realm

of the private joke

—sometimes my favourite realm.

Are you with me? There's no point. I can't
make sense much longer—
Cochise?
—Who, me?
Yes. Take this nail & hit it into my forehead.

Firmly.
—You crazy, boss!
When
I feel like this I read the poems of Ron Padgett
—NO OFFENCE!—
I jump down, turn around
pick a bale of cotton

A little wine in the morning,
a little breakfast at night.

Where *is* the great
but absent art of our age. Giles Auty,
huh?

Take your hands out of your pockets when you
talk to me, son!

Crusty old fool
you sketchy cruiser

To the right of the critic—the picture is on the left,
large, smudged—to *the right* the wainscot drifts away
& becomes, after a passage of irresolute drawing,
sand—there stands the figure of Napoleon.
And he is in one helluva mood, as always. His

function is purely allegorical—as we must point out
to him. He represents the mood
of Mr Auty, on a relatively bad day—the tide of history,
the impoverished taste of most of this century. What
am I even *doing* in this allegory, he thinks—
Napoleon *is drawn weakly, as if by*
some amateur—say Victor Hugo,
inspired but easy, an idea, *not a figure observed.*
Though it's Napoleon alright, & stormy clouds of brushed ink
loom immediately right of him, ineptly complementing
the vague grey,
at left, of *the erased de Kooning*.

Further right—
what is this, a bad dream!?—some vacant fool like
Larry Rivers is fucking a chair. Must I be
associated with this? What is this called,
An Allegorical Disparaging of Giles Auty? Yep.

The Raft of the Medusa.

. . . for me the rot sets in sometime after Delacroix—
he had colour. Ingres had "the probity of drawing".
But look at Chassériau . . . & then
the Symbolists came along & it's been downhill
ever since. That dill for instance—Puvis de
Chavannes!

& yet, could we have had Gauguin
without him? I would prefer to.

Just as I would
prefer the late Derain without the earlier—
though *that is his whole point*. Why couldn't Bonnard
be stronger—couldn't he see where it led?

Hard to approve the politics of David,
or even Caravaggio—a lout probably—I can't see him
reading *The Spectator*. Was there no one round
like me to listen to? Or is that the point, not listening?
The whole thing becomes pretty terminally ill
with Duchamp. Just look at the deleterious effects
his permission had on lesser talents—Picabia, Arp—
though this gives Duchamp credit for talent
he never had.

It leads directly to all this nonsense with
Sherrie Levine, Daniel Buren—art as
mere conceptual gesture—in this country John Nixon,
the idiotic self portraits of Mike Parr (drawn as if
from a funny angle—what is the point of the
anamorphosis, somewhere different to stand in the gallery?
squinting, backing into sculpture?), the grandiosities
of Imants Tillers. *Young man, the academicians*
were right! Look at Sickert—& go back from there,
being selective, avoiding the mistakes of Turner, for what
was good about him, yet not so far as Poussin; Velasquez
was a high point, if only generous in very small measure.
Hard men, he & I. Let me introduce myself,
Giles Auty—my eyes narrowed, my jaw firm—doomed
to wander, through time, homeless, a brooding figure,
part Naploeon, part Goofy, caped. I'm right. You
do know that. I used to write for *The Spectator.*

Johann Winckelmann

Notes

- "A marked decline in deference". This decline the *Spectator* noted as it became apparent to even *its* readers that John Major's Tories would be defeated at the next election. The *Spectator* is home to Peregrine Worsthorne, Auberon Waugh & others of Auty's ilk who've been trotted out to the colonies from time to time—to ginger things up with their ebullient views.
- "I think continually of those who were truly great"—a line from Spender, I think.
- Robert Rauschenberg erased a de Kooning drawing—a kind of 'significant gesture' ironising the gestural artist's endeavour, erasing it, doubling it etc.
- Cy Twombly—the odd, but not so odd, monicker of a European-based US artist whose works are often described as pure mark-making, codeless meaning, automatism, & delectable, moody & poignant.
- *Scribble, scribble, scribble—eh Mr Gibbon!*—King George's response to Gibbon upon publication of the latter's *Decline & Fall.*
- Donald Brook—cool & mocking doubter of all things expressionistic, transcendent & idealist in art—in fact rather doubtful of art itself. Excepting 'art-as-properly-so-called'.
- Cochise—in this poem the American Indian—*any* American Indian—as traduced by that country's cowboy-&-injun movies of the 50s, once a staple of daytime TV.
- Ron Padgett—in many ways the leading US poet of his generation.
- from "jump down, turn around" to "hands out of your pocket" are quoted, respectively, Leadbelly, Lou Reed, Clement Greenberg, Otis Spann.
- "Crusty old fool, sketchy cruiser"—Adelaide teen street argot, circa 1997.

- Victor Hugo—people forget the windbag's efforts as watercolorist & draughtsperson.
- "fucking a chair"—Larry Rivers, perhaps the leading US artist of his generation: a later work represents (i.e., depicts) this harmless adolescent activity of the artist's.
- *An Allegorical Disparaging of Giles Auty*—I think this must be the alternative title or job description of the poem—though "Allegorical" aspires to airs.
- *The Wreck of the Medusa*—why do people unfailingly say 'Raft'?—is a painting by Gericault.
- Delacroix—had colour.
- Ingres—had the probity of drawing. (Or was drawing "the crucible of his style"?)
- Chassériau—tried some of both. (These entries are sourced from *The Dictionary Of Received Ideas*.)
- Puvis (de Chavannes)—solemn, hilarious, he had something though.
- Gauguin—was played by Anthony Quinn in that movie about the life of the other guy.
- Derain—part of the Return to Order.
- David—Jacques Louis David, hot-head radical.
- Caravaggio—we actually know that Caravaggio subscribed in his Roman years (nothing is known certainly of those following) to *The Lanced Tumour Review*, *We're Dirt* & *Easy Chicken*. Caravaggio contributed, too, to the second & third issues of *Modern Painters*—in the first a *letter from Parma* & in the second a *letter from Venice* (though he is not thought to have visited Venice). For these he appears never to have been paid.
- "Sculpture?—something you back into while looking at painting."—Ad Reinhardt's view. Actually he had backed into the critic, Hilton Kramer.
- Auty "protests too much"? (Shakespeare) I'm not so sure Auty did write for the *Spectator*.

(Two Portraits)

down amongst this pile of books by the bed
the bottom of a magazine sticks out, as it
has for some weeks now, announcing "Chuck Close"
—an exhibition—& consequently, if briefly, I think of him,
a career I know almost
nothing about: one portrait, that resembles

the IRA's Gerry Adams, but which—more, presumably—resembles
Close himself. Also by the bed
another's portrait, someone I *have* met—almost
diaphanous, evanescent, in the photo. I met the poet it
depicts years after it was taken. Tony Towle. It seems therefore
magical & fictive, like a fable *about* him—
a fable he has been cast in—relative to the solidity of the few facts
that, for me, say, constitute Close.

A more recent image of Chuck Close—
a photo—has him in a wheelchair. He is painting, & it resembles
that same portrait, so I take it that it *was* him
all those years ago—done in grids, pixellated in appearance, looming
over artist, wheelchair, bed,
table-with-brushes—though (in greys) it could almost,
or *easily*, be a drawing. It

suggests some struggle, this photo, . . . heroism . . . True, it
is something I hadn't known about Chuck Close.
For seconds each night, regularly almost—
though subliminally until today—*which*, irritatingly, resembles

suddenly the day before it, in that again for some seconds this
        morning, in bed,
unwillingly I entertain my only two images of him—

they 'pop up': & once more I dwell on them—on him—
(or don't) momentarily. It
is my memory's almost empty file on Chuck Close—&, in bed,
unwanted, it makes itself available to me. Normally it wouldn't, and
        thinking of Close
I think pretty immediately of Thomas Ruff, whose work his resembles—
the German photographer, in large format, of faces & streets. While I
        have almost

never thought about the American I have thought about Ruff—who almost
came to Australia, I think: someone phoned once to ask should we bring him.
Out of regret that I didn't push harder I've attended to Ruff ever since. All of
        which in no way resembles
my feelings for this other portrait—a poet whose work I love, so that it
is pure good faith, this relationship. The 'cool' of the early Close
I found unimpressive, & ugly—in a fashionable way, whose fashionability I
        wasn't buying. Chuck's by the bed

by accident, a name only. By contrast, the poems are there permanently. It
is the poet's *Selected*, now out of print. On it Towle resembles other pictures
        I have seen of him,
though this is the most curious. He might almost have borrowed the coat he
        wears. He will regret, amusedly, his hair. The guileless heroism of
        the smile, the eyes, he will not regret. But the poems I keep close

he might have wanted more for. I grant Close
the pathos of the new works—though I have only experienced it via
magazine pages, one or two pictures . . .

Then, Minimalism & Pop 'had had their day'
as things new & imperative. I didn't find them
(or him), in '74, inherently compelling. Not the way

I found about the same time, say, Tuckson, Robert Ryman. (In this 'indirect'
way
guilt maintains a close connection between me and a particular sub-set of
art works. As close
or closer than between me and works I've liked probably. I remember them
ruefully: a history of opinions—mine—via
mistakes I might have made.) Literalism was my big thing. Will the
day
come when it is not? I'm not sure it still isn't—the pictures

on the back of Towle's books regarding me quizzically as I say it—pictures
in which his face has altered from a kind of resolute simplicity, looking
the way
David would paint Napoleon say, towards a more casually raffish, day-
at-the-office pose: open collar, hair tousled, the close
New York weather (tho Larry Rivers' artwork suggests Via
dei Carrottieri, Via del Corso . . . a coffee shop or bar on one of them,

—or an Italianate church or library as setting) . . . the weather plasters
strips of hair to the forehead. Near them
the hand upon which the head rests, the face looking at us, amused
though withdrawn. The pictures
never tell us who is in that gaze—though of one we know, via
a poem he wrote, that he wondered would people assume—as they made
their way
past him—he was famous? & would the smoke appear, as it blew close
by (from left to right, I guess, as we look at the photo)? It doesn't. One
imagines him that day

stepping out of his office for the portrait—unfairly less certain of fame, or
knowing that one day
his name would make one of a minor configuration of names. People would
read them
and a certain New York charm, wistfulness, way of life would be
evoked—the close
of the century, the American century perhaps. Of all the various pictures
I have of New York, mentally, those I like best are intimately architectural,
way
more domestic than skyscrapers. —Footpaths; leaves; shop-fronts: images
gained via

TV shows—but also my one trip there, and Tony Towle's poems; the
connecting shots, where we move, via
the coffee shop, to Jerry's apartment, to Elaine's new boyfriend's. Night in
Towle pertains always to New York, for me, but day
can be either New York's apartments, streets . . . or a kind of dazzling,
elating, studio-lit clarity—that plays over Tiepolo's clouds, de
Chirico's white horses & crazed senators, way-
laid armchairs, pillars & pilasters—neoclassical, absurdly ornamented.
While *this* is true of them
the poems are also restful, airy. Poems immensely civilized. Noble,
grandiloquent—& amusingly indirect as method. Like Close's pictures
they are large, but they are gestures of self-effacement, miming a kind of
huge Romantic pathos: self-directed irony—but a *fictive* self, the
formally preserved reticence as to the real self its single enormous
gesture. Large—like the Close

portrait with its squared, detachedly close-rendered sheets of detail: the big
identity conveyed via
isolated fragments, all attention to technique. The artist's single pictures
locate one seeming moment of a day,

typically the moment that begins or ends it, in a mirror. The poems say more, do more, pass lightly, even, over the moments of portraiture or exaggerate them terribly. Except on the back cover, the poet, to be seen, looks away.

Three Poems For John Forbes

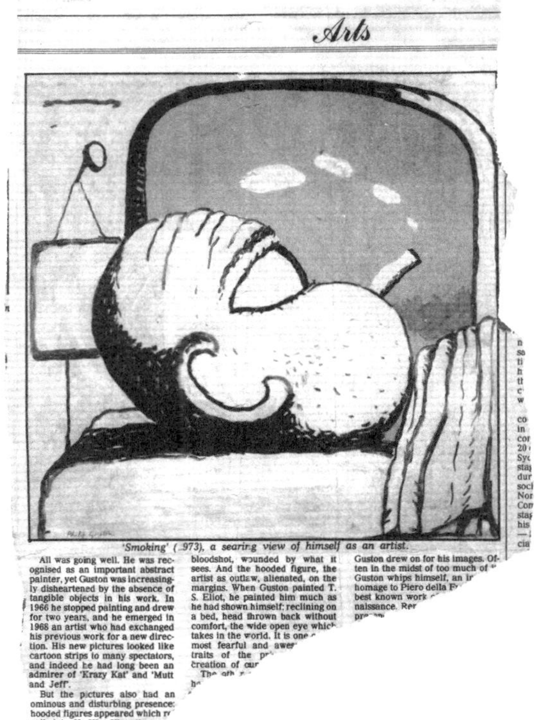

Arts

'Smoking' (_973), a searing view of himself as an artist.

All was going well. He was recognised as an important abstract painter, yet Guston was increasingly disheartened by the absence of tangible objects in his work. In 1966 he stopped painting and drew for two years, and he emerged in 1968 an artist who had exchanged his previous work for a new direction. His new pictures looked like cartoon strips to many spectators, and indeed he had long been an admirer of 'Krazy Kat' and 'Mutt and Jeff'.

But the pictures also had an ominous and disturbing presence: hooded figures appeared which r... Ku Klux Klan; they ...

bloodshot, wounded by what it sees. And the hooded figure, the artist as outlaw, alienated, on the margins. When Guston painted T. S. Eliot, he painted him much as he had shown himself: reclining on a bed, head thrown back without comfort, the wide open eye which takes in the world. It is one ... most fearful and awe... traits of the ... creation of ...

Guston drew on for his images. Often in the midst of too much of ... Guston whips himself, an ... homage to Piero della F... best known work ... naissance. Re...

Coffee & John Forbes Poem

Funny, the Guston selfportrait
I always associated with myself
I associate with you—"he
became his admirers"
not much of a fate
for you in my case.
Your new book is out
I'm reading it in
exactly the place you'd have
imagined me in—a
nondescript Adelaide coffee shop
your picture of me too cruelly true
—well, not "cruelly", but "true"—
taking the world in manageable bites:
there was me, there was the
art world (I knew all the artists)
there was Poetry—an idea
I held in my head—
there was politics in the papers
& out the windows Hindley Street—
reality, the
'modern world'—
I could have a think
maybe a bit of a write
putting things, keeping things,
in their place.
                    The new poems
are great. But that's it
the end of the supply—

poems that as they came along
seemed admonitions, a wake-up call—
& we rose or didn't
to the occasion
knowing there'd be more,
thinking of you. I pictured
you, typically, in late night concentration—
in your place, rather barren
a naked light maybe over you—
your head, your glasses, a
T-shirt, maybe TV going
in the corner—the sound down
behind you. Was it like that?
I feel like phoning Gig—
saying what *did* he look like
there writing?
                    Late at night?
in the morning? kitchen table?
did he face the wall, the
fireplace?
I visited—once or
twice—
I remember the scene.
He liked it. It was not what you would call
'comfortable'.

                    The young look cute to me
just for being young. A couple
walks by her hand for warmth
in his hippocket, arms around each other.
John saw them
as he saw everything maybe

more accurately. I don’t know.
I think it’ll be weird—
those wake-up calls that were
the poems will now come to seem
a period, a ‘moment’ as we
Marxists say (parentheses here for
har har) now passed—
to which Australian poetry
never responded.

Hi, John

in the lecture The Idea of The City / Modernity / The Suburban Mall I plan to quote my favourite poets

but find I am looking out the window
looking up from the cream of the paper—

green leaves, ivy-covered tin
(of the fence some feet away), but mostly

rust, & darker brown: leaves—
unswept, on the brick & at the base of the olive tree—the

ancient plum whose
leaves & arthritic black limbs

frame this, I think. A bird moves maybe
or the sun shines, intermittently,

that little bit brighter.
I look again at various poems that,

as it happens, could be
models for talking of you—though

in each case
I doubt if I could do it,

sustain the particular sort of beauty
possessed in the original.

It's interesting—or is it,
is it just adventitious?—

that beauty is the desired effect.
Maybe it is fair enough—

a number of your poems
achieved such grace

&, as well,

beauty seems the kind of
balm that should

be offered the lack you felt—
recognition withheld.

                                        This seems not
to be that poem. Not beautiful.

But that's me, as you
might point out, *not you*. In fact

I did point it out. *I* do all
the talking here.

I'm alone—as are
others, your friends—in my case

with the curious goad
of many of the poems before me

you loved, I'd guess. "Buried At Springs", "Salute",
Berrigan's, Frank's. Whom it is always

weird calling that. Tho
'the literature'

encourages it. And odd—
when I had not got very used

to referring to *you* as "John".
You were in my thoughts a lot

in later years. And were John then,
and are—alternately—

both now: the fearsomely good
poet designated by the surname,

& "John"—the pleasure in your
remarks, gratitude for late night

phone calls: a review I'd written,
some idea I'd like—our concern,

finally, for your own cares.

When I said goodnight to you—'composed'
beneath a 40 watt bulb, on a sagging camp bed—

the doctor having told you you might die,
it was hard not to be amused

as well as worried: you wouldn't die
of course, but would you be well?
                                                  (The doctor,

we took it, putting the frighteners
on you.) Anna, twelve,

resembled you
a few weeks ago—

conked-out, the TV going,
a blanket pulled high,

her round, angelic head,
her buried chin. The term

that mediates or bridges
her image & yours

a Guston picture, of a head smoking
(*called* "Smoking"),

its eyes wide, a profile, worried.
And then you died.

I wonder when I will die?
Though if you came back

it would not be to talk about
that, but to admire

some certain turn of phrase,
or—you being you—

the compressed but
pivotal implication

in something you had seen—
something of mine

if you were being generous,
some point purchased

with the concomitant faults
attendant on it—

in *my* writing at any rate, not
in yours.

          Since I've mentioned
Anna you'd ask
after her (she's going great)

& Gabe & Kim
(them too)
                    —as you always did.

Tho I would be impatient
for the literary talk

that (in any case)
I didn't do well.

It was a calming sort of thing,
to talk about them:

the kids you seemed to find
both an irritant and

hope-giving sign
of things to come:

miraculous youth.
You enjoyed their energy, the

connection of mind to
body, the reflexes, the hormones—the promise.

Then we'd rabbit on.
(Poetry.) Now we must all attempt

to do that for each other, your friends.
You're gone. I listened

to a tape of you a few days ago.
One I forgot I had.

Spot on.

Muddy Waters relaxing between gigs — photograph © Val Wilmer

Girls Watching Movie, Palace Theater, ca. 1943 Weegee (Arthur Fellig)
Gelatin silver print © Weegee / International Center of Photography / Getty Images

People Passing Time

On the wall
pictures of people passing time
Young girls
photographed   by Weegee
at the movies
Sleeping,
lying on each other, blowing gum,
bored,

transfixed

— at the spectacle   probably
of Adult Life
presented to them
Muddy Waters
— *in the other pic* —
playing cards
About to snap one down,
smiling
in the pic
John wrote about
John who is dead
As is Muddy
As are the girls
probably
Dead or dying
photographed in 1942
migrant
New Yorkers

their human, evaluating faces

As is Guston
who has painted his own head
a rounded cartoon in profile
eyes wide, smoking
staring sightless
at a ceiling,
at his life . . .

But not me yet
& I've
"got a drawing to do"
for Micky Allan

. . . Late at night
& passing time

an old tape
music

So my time passed
which was given me upon earth
as Brecht & Eisler said
dead too
O sky of streaming
azure blue
Micky,
is *this* any good?

does drawing.

It's too late, too late—
Too late   too late   too late

I'm on my way to Denver
& I cannot hesitate

Joe Turner said that.

Anyway,
I've tried everything I could / just to get along with you

& now I've done this drawing

It shows the Five Basic
Attitudes   to life
considered as a problem
— *Sleep*
Rapt attention,
Boredom,
Intelligent appraisal
(after all, this may happen to you
best
to have an
opinion)
& Half aghast
(—could Life
'be'
so *Mean*?)

girl puts knuckles in

her mouth

against her face

protection

consolation

Where

Where

where, will you *be* tonight ?

In a *world* of trouble says Joe.

I say I've

got the main girl right

The others are just shapes, but you

get the idea

Don't you

'Too cute!'

I hear John say from the grave

The basic attitude.

I wonder whose voice said those things to John

in

his mind?

Gig's? Laurie's? Mine, maybe,

on occasion.

His speaks to mine

— as alive

as always —

#

His was alive

mine was asleep
dozing
like a very quiet limb
his supply of
bon mots
was amazing

I've pronounced that
"motts"

by the way
disfiguring the poem
—tho it sounds
'better' that way

just as I've disfigured the drawing
but
the main girl

is okay
& the scribble I've added,
left,
fixes it.
What would a *similar* shading be   for the poem—

some classical allusion
about John, the poet, 'from the
grave'   etc
—something moving

Like my last

picture of John

that resembles the Guston

composed on his bed

contemplating

death

Tho *I* didn't think he would die

nor did he, maybe

John, forgive me for being a jerk

#

Not that there's any point

saying it now

God, this will bring me down.

#

Time,

maybe, to write to Laurie

The 'late' Sam Cooke is

singing

'live' "For Sentimental Reasons".

—'Very funny'.

but I don't care
& not too cute
I am like the girl now,
blowing gum.   Life.   God, I'm glad I live in a century
with electric light.

Jesus,
it occurs to me to say something
really horrible

. . . but I won't

The fluoro desk lamp
when I sit back   makes a great white diagonal
against the dark blue
of the curtains

Which drape like *Renaissance* drapery
(or Baroque)
tho they drape mostly
over
jars of pencils
pencil cases I never open
'desk furniture'

that has collected against the window ledge.
Nearer,
the mess of papers, folders
— books
watch, toothpicks
biro caps
a cup   a yoghurt container —

that fill the
rest.
'Bernini'
(the curtain) —
& this contemporary detritus

Brilliantly   lit
More comforting than lovely
My
attention to it   meaning
like John was
I'm alive.

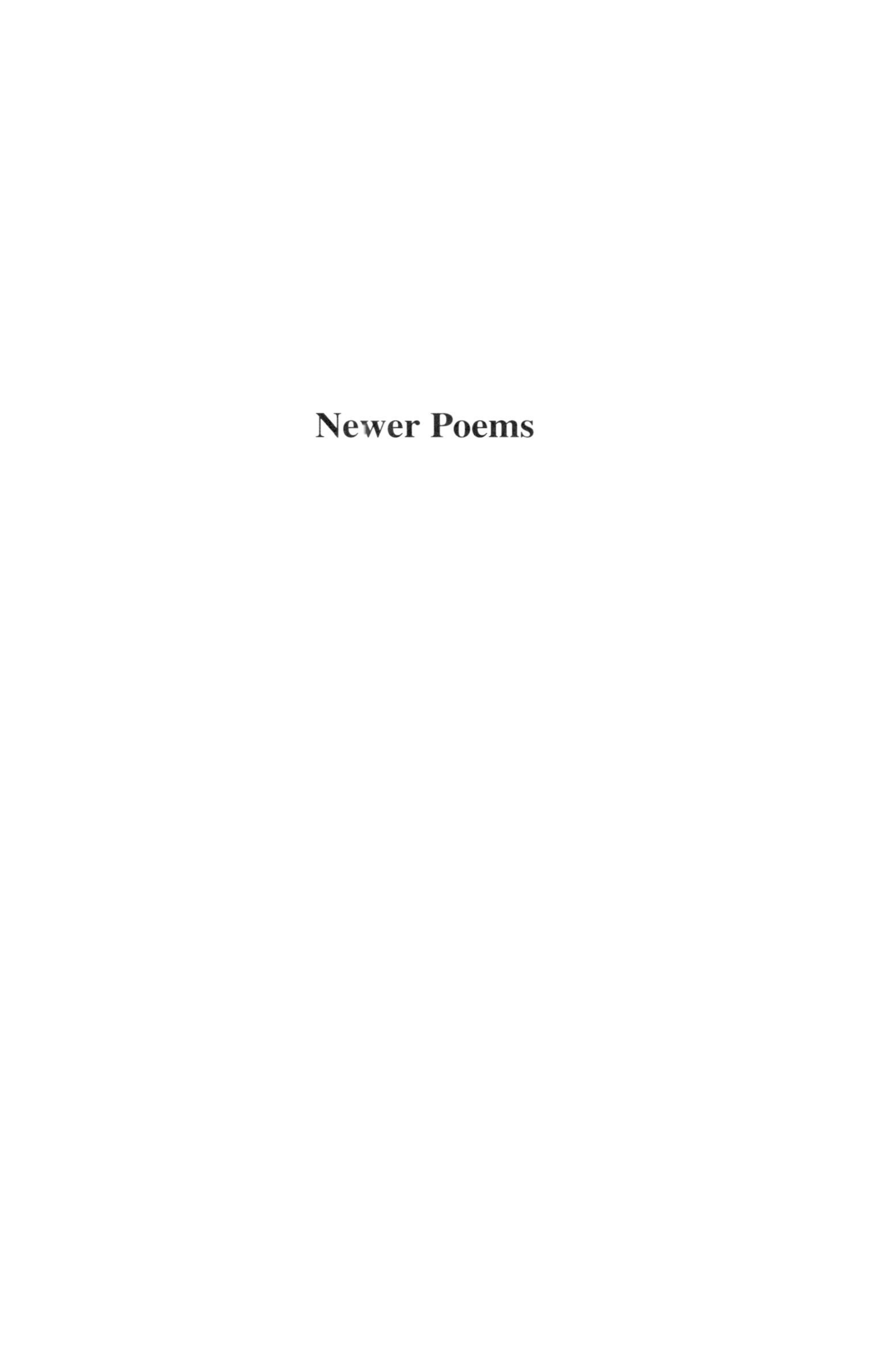

Newer Poems

Your Being Away

I'm searching for—I guess—a minor Frank O'Hara
poem
a late one   whose name I can't remember.
                                                            Not one

I should find
                    Too sentimental perhaps to bring out
my best
            But one I'm in the mood for.
                                                                    And isn't
that
      why we write poems occasionally?—
                                                            not responsibly but
anyhow?
            The late hour
                              & a cigarette
                                                            have made me
sensitive to sound
                    I think
                              so my ears ring with the
silence
            John Pilger & Pam Brown
                                                            enjoin me
Not to be sentimental

                                                      or at least to be
sharp
            Cath's daughter, Anna,
                                                gone to bed,

Cath
away—
for tonight,
& the next
& Gabe
completing an assignment
before catching a plane—
& flying to the bars & surf,
monkeys
etcetera
of Indonesia—
dishes done,
dinner cooked—
NATO bombing in Kosovo;
a program
on the Warsaw
ghetto—

What will I be sentimental *about*?

"He says
'hello',"
—to quote the poem,
which I've found—

" 'this is
George Gordon, Lord Byron' "
—Frank speaking on the phone
to a loved one.
Byron liked the Albanians, I know.

"And for once it is not three in the morning,"

(the poem
says next)
Tho for me
it almost is. For Frank
I think he
meant
it wasn't his usual late night call, tired &
emotional.

I am
not on the phone.
Tomorrow.

Tomorrow I will call.
'He'—the poem has the first person
transposed to "he" throughout—

he, in my case, will be
especially moved
to see *her*
(who is you)—

tho only a day or two removal
is all there will be—
enough to constitute 'me'
as lonely,
or *alone*,
tho pleasantly—
dreaming of you, your finely nerved,
beautiful & expressive face—
on the pillow, or,

characteristically, reading,
the eyes so liquid
drinking the book in
intelligently:
happy to watch
your intelligence,
more balanced more calm
more
finely tuned than 'his'
(mine),
except when watching you

—To sleep, now
(or—as I'm staying up—*later*)
"protected
only by your love"

Poem ('Cat-Bag')

down the back
the light is on
so my dad
—if he wakes—can see.

The rain,
beating down creates
a kind of silence, a sound
that blankets all the others—fridge,
fluoro light—
a bubble
in which I work,
sit really

seeking to avoid cliché—
& thus reduced to silence

A review
in front of me that I
don't want to write.

The poems
of a poet I admire—full of things
that *it's*
alright for him *to say*

(That is,
"but I *can't"*.)

A big selection
of Samuel Johnson   to fall back on—
to pass the time

It is interesting
how it would change things if I named
the other poet

"Interesting"? how is
that used here?   *shouldn't* it
be interesting, the consequence of
what you say?
Or are these
paths one merely "assents" to,

as in—
"not down that path again"?—
to quote a poem of mine & John's.
Solipsism the only integrity.

Cath comes out—
squeak of door to the hall—
appears walking scrunched a little,
eyes scrunched, half-closed
to remain asleep. Bathroom, &
back to bed. We talk a little.

The Banana grows older each week
& tonight came in to say goodnight,
Cath already asleep, so
she said it anyway & asked *me*
to come & check on her (instead)

"in ten" & when I did
it was dark, her radio going
quietly—"Are you asleep?" *"Nearly—*
what do you want?" "Your ten minutes.
You said to check. You alright?"
"Yep." "See you in the morning." All
of this whispered. Sort of amusing.
In fact I'd told her *she* should
come back in ten & check on Cath—
but a joke I'd told before. Now
I get some water for Cath & say
goodnight, again, to her,
                                        & read:
Samuel Johnson, or the poet—Jimmy
Schuyler.

There, that's the cat out of that bag.

                                        What
do other people do with their time—
smoke, watch TV, get on the phone?—
I mean, time like this?
They look for poetry like *you* write, Ken.
Joke. Point
taken. Integrity again, a
careful system of checks &
balances—joke again, tho
the point of the joke is lost on
someone slow as me,
tho its form I recognize.
It was my joke of course.

I wrote a
poem once that said "Chuck-chuck
chuckling thru the Night." Doesn't
the word "joke" appear a lot (above)?
& the word "again"? Doesn't it
tell you something? I suppose it
does—time to smile now,
ruefully. Tho on another night
I'll be laughing, up late, spinning
records (tapes, vinyl—*CDs* if
I'm in this room), reading books,
daydreaming
strap-hanging—on
the train that is my life
as it takes me to my destination, the
light & dark of the stations meanwhile
flashing by

now
I read
"The Walk"
the lines
so slim
& delicate
the timing
almost ec-
statically quiet
so great it
caps the night.

Extinguished,
I crash out.

American Friends

"I am ashamed of my century
for being so entertaining
but I have to smile"—Frank O'Hara

Ah nuts! It's boring reading English newspapers
in Adelaide as if I were a Colonial waiting for my gin
somewhere beyond this roof a jet is making a sketch of the sky
where is Laurie Duggan I wonder if he's reading under a dwarf pine
stretched out so his book & his head fit under the lowest branch
while the great southland sun rolls calmly not getting thru to him
not caring particularly tho the light in Sydney does not get

to see so many poets, while in Blackheath or Marrickville
Pam—particle or wave theory?—divides her time
between them, reads Eileen Myles or Susan Schultz
(American friends) everybody here is running around or sitting tight &
being grim I once saw Laurie swim 'backstroke'—so he motored
feet first around a pool I dreamed I saw Pam
in a play I never wrote—wave theory
might explain this, crazy, intense, the picture ghosting

inexplicable Steve Kelen where is he, *et famille*? In Viet Nam?
Adam, where him? I emailed but did not look
to see where. Back soon. Alan is in Honkers
Dipti in Melbourne Richard & Suzy are in New York
buying the CDs that will fill out his collection—*that* is culture
right? & maybe making art did I see Jenny Watson's painting of
herself
sleeping in New York in New York? If I did will Suzy see it? a
bed in Central Park. Susan Hiller calls & sees them

who would be so New York, wouldn't she, in New York? the way
she didn't seem in Adelaide tho exotic, sure, an

American friend—Dennis Hopper was the American Friend
when I first saw it a washed-up American almost,
a mercenary, like the character, an American 'for hire' which made it seem
subversive or sophisticated, the use of him. My American Friend here
is O'Hara so I expect that I am subverted
I expect the charge—in any case—I deal with him again
to see can I gain advantage poetically Surely if I get
out of my depth Frank who was by many accounts
quite a swimmer can come powering thru the surf
to save me as the life saver does now for a little kid
'in difficulties' amongst the many bods & standing figures & figures
swimming
round her—like me, with Laurie, Pam, Adam
(who lives by a beach). Horseshoe Bay, Pt Eliot is where I am,

whereas Adam when he gets back gets back to Bondi,
a real beach. The lifesaver carries the curly-headed girl—
aged 8, aged 5?—to the very edge of the sand, under one arm,
above his hip, jokingly & places her in the wet sand
where the surf just reaches as she runs away from him
& up the beach no doubt relieved or filled with an
adventure
to tell
where are my friends—
having adventures?
do
they picture me, & as I am, writing this, sitting
in the shade at a beach, the cries of kids, mild,
thinking of them?

I can't help noticing
how wrong
O'Hara's opinions about this
American Century
have turned out to be
& remembering
how much I liked them
tho they were wrong then
they were wrong
even when he wrote them—like Dennis Hopper in the film
wishing it were not so

So here I am,
protective of these opinions for being even
as blithe as they are but you are the American, wrong—
even here, in this client state, my hero

Horizon

"In this dawn as in the first
it's the Homeric rose, its scent
that leads on"
—Frank O'Hara,
'Ode to Willem de Kooning'

"As a people we are now called
Australians because a vast & lonely land
has touched us with her differences"
—George Ivan Smith,
1953 preface to *For The Term Of His Natural Life*

"it's noble to refuse to be
added up or divided"
—Frank O'Hara

"Beyond the sunrise
where the black begins"—
& the lights of the city, we
imagine, twinkle or blaze . . .

the horizon line here
a curve of butter yellow,
slightly oxidized—lined,
at its rim, by olive-green 'natives'—
hides a city that if I am
facing the right way
must be doing its afternoon trade
relaxed this last few days after December 25th

but ready nonetheless for the big push
at night, the raid on
fun desire release—
selling mostly coffee, wine,
Michael / rolls a joint *has* one
then rolls several others children
contemplate navels—the girls their own
with quiet pride, the boys the girls'
with longing puzzling as it is strong
Mary paints her nails, reads, Cuban music
playing. What of Margaret, of Crab? they do
those things normative in a utopia
a cork is popped, Marg plays
fado, the soulful music of Portugal
or Crab practises on sax
reads some politics, some mayhem, reads
the poems I gave him. *I*
try to seize upon that greatness
which is available to me
if it is available at all
(am I facing the right way?)
thru art.
                    The view is
quintessentially Australian, which is its
problem—for me—tho not classical
& in its particulars
is information (where the classic typically presents
only sign). The essays of
Meaghan are to hand which might
stiffen my resolve or form it: *not to be*
inimitably weak & picturesque myself
but standing forth a subject not a spectacle.

There are daisies nearby & a shin-high wall
of loose but flat-laid shale or slate twelve feet
beyond—a standard country wire fence; the
field of grass; on the horizon a distinct
curve of hill three hundred yards away, a
water tank nestles in to the furthest reach
of the olive 'natives'—
can I drop the scare marks from
that word now, hasn't it
done enough? &
I rest their case
                    "for now
a long history slinks
over the sill",
                    & with it history's ironies, reversals
sarcasms so *de rigueur*. I never wanted to be postcolonial
or colonial just modern which is
the joke on me—but who wants to be a category?
Many would be right—it will do me to be interested—&
one accepts the truth like a tired disguise handed out
for the party—is this me?—& joins the crowd
as the brave must always ascend, always the musts:
the Eiffel tower, the flight over London, the café
table—in Rundle Street or rue de la Rocquette
where Lorraine lived & we stayed tho for me, today,
this hill is my focus, the clouds—(for I must ascend)—
are beautiful & white & echoing fluidly the hills'
shape, the splotches of green that mottle the yellow
& remind of 'Minor Moderns of South Australia'
a line I join of precursors—Horace Trennery,
Dorritt Black—pondering a relation
to the minor English, Europe, the

universal—& its status as 'the wrong question'
which strolls now & then into a field
& sits down like a forgotten rock
while 'we' walk on
to an horizon line, that's beautiful, keen,
precarious, & doesn't tug—not 'rose', but
serene, & melancholy, & joyous, all at the same time, a kind
of benediction that says, I'm free & I'm gratuitous
why not feel better? & since you do you do
return: into that inanimate world of voices cross-
questioning you, no longer like your father, a man
in an open necked shirt eating an icecream (& just,
perhaps, 'going for a walk'), but in a shirt I bought in Melbourne
made by migrant Vietnamese late at night, yet in which
I feel Australian, whatever that is
                                        —a point mapped by coordinates
you momentarily 'keep your eye on', or don't, being
yourself or a moving target (do the hills you climb as
no one count? The hostess explains,
As we leave administered life
there is a slight discomfort—the tug of
gravity on re-entry returns, you may
feel tired. *Where*, the open neck shirted men, women in
thongs & sandals, ask *is our shimmering ideal?* If O'Hara
had such timing John his last move suggests he blew it
Tho exits are notoriously hard to make. "I live above a
dyke bar & I'm happy"—I might too for all I know.
Am *I*? Occasionally, occasionally *very*. The female
of the tiny blue jay or 'wren' appears, bouncing,
across the grass outside then some of the 'men' &
move across my field of view from left to right . . .

Catching Up With Kurt Brereton

Hi Kurt.
(!) I'm sitting up
(here)
(at night)
the Pharoah Sanders I bought while staying
with you playing
gentle mania
waxing waning
*
quietly doing its nut

*

(in the corner)
*
"Is Sal alright?" my main question
That I should ask her
My question to you :
"What's doing?"
Right now, a Sunday night,
will you be stretching the weekend: music spinning . . .
lighting a number, painting,
making notes on things
the fish zipping about, watching you, saying
I hope he plays the James Reyne tape again?
But fish—what would they know?
their
red & blue, flickering, the bubbles rising out of that diver,
paintings of swimmers
—humanity at its rare least guarded—

around.
'Around'!
what are you floating about like
that—
get back with the other swimmers!
Ya wanna know
what I think? in Peggy's words

("Nick,
ya wanna know what I think?"
"Hey, *Nick!* . . ." Etcetera.)

A mantra
*
I should ring you
*

but don't know where
the phone will ring—
in the house

If it was to hand
in the studio & you picked it up on just two rings
& said, mellow & unphased,
Yeah?
that would be
the greatest thing

(am I *stoned*?)

what is this thing
with being stoned—I,

who almost never come out of
my tree
except by coaxing myself down—
a coffee, a
long quiet night?
Like *Krazy Kat* now
I stand
at the foot of that tree (in fact a lamp post
incredibly
tall
a foot or two beyond the perimeter of its
light
(its penumbra)

pretty benign
charmed

(by my *'own song'*)
big-eyed
—dumb, yeah,
but what's new—
"I never said I was smart"
to quote Lou Reed
Actually, Lou said "tasteful"
If he can lie
why can't I?
'Smart', eh?
Then
time to
attempt it
I pick up the phone
& dial you

Hello?

I do a drawing, standing, at my desk,

a hat near some papers & jars & a jar of flowers—

#

looking down.

#

Keeps me going for an hour

#

& call it "August 6th" tho it's April

& years

later

. . . & the poem I do it for

was probably

not written on August 6th either

the months just have

such evocative names,

Of *what* are they evocative?

just evocative, that's all :

leaves, sky, weather

This hat

on which I look down—

so

definite,

so casual—

suggests to me scotch

tho I have none now—

& the races, gambling,

A masculine world

the adult world of my father

A flat in Elizabeth Bay
                                        frangipanis, the harbour

where Sal & Laurie live

                                    The light from the lamp
gives a thin firm shadow
round its brim, on one side—
                                        which my charcoal seizes
other details drop out
                                    & as I draw & look
& draw again
                    it is 1951—the humidity,   the slight
sweatyness of Sydney
                                    I feel tough & gentle
calm
                    It is the nostalgia of the style,
                                                    the hat
the flower: the flower pink & pale—hibiscus—
against dark green leaves, the jar small &
six-sided   the hat is wheaten yellow straw, with
a band of brown   the harsh light of the lamp
whitening everything—sheets of paper, bits of writing,
a pen, pencils
                    the drink this all suggests
is nowhere to be found an absence that keeps the whole
                            unsettled
provisional   suggesting a *moment*, not an hour

I get two long-necked bottles from the fridge, put them
in a bag & catch a tram up the Cross meet Cath Pam
Sal & Laurie & continue down the beach

where we meet
you
near where you lived forty-five years later
I'm not
wearing a hat, & neither are you, tho Laurie is
aside
from that everyone is dressed pretty much as normal—
classic,
eh?   Pam has a rollie
Sal an *Ardath*
I rub Cath's neck simultaneously in 1951 & now
& Rosemary hands you the corkscrew, whose handle is a
bottle-opener, & Sarah & Laurie hold out glasses—
beer really was beer till some time in the seventies—
Laurie says *Well, cheers!* & we clink the glasses

Traffic Noises, Cups, Voices

"What are you doing here? Shouldn't
you be in Rome?"
—Tony Kirkman

I can remember coming here
for the first time, when *The Flash* moved
from its old spot across the street.
Larger, brighter, it was a week
or two, or three, before the move

was not sharply regretted. Jules
declared the new *Flash* off her round
so severely did it lack the
charm the old possessed—the
hole-in-the-wall, small town

refusal of economies
of scale, 50s / 60s pale green
walls, every booth filled more or less
by six or seven regulars,
older Italians who'd been

there every day for years—which made
lucking-out and getting a spot
a privilege. Incognito
one sat in silence, espresso,
paper, book, sunglasses on or off

the balm of being out-of-time—
    The Cone Of Silence descending
around you. Suddenly what had
often been the chief complaint had
    been transformed in remembering

to a virtue. The clatter—and
    sometimes pandemonium—of
The Flash not much changed. When did
it move? Who cares? (Years ago—six,
    eight.) She is reminiscent of

Julie, this waitress, though with less
    idea of makeup—Julie would
point out—and I'd agree. Less hip.
A man watching women. Let this
    not be one of those poems. Could

I be said to do anything else?
    Watching people. E.G., I never think
of the cosmos. Though politics,
philosophy I read. The trick
    is the sudden fit—*lack* of fit—

then fit again, of enormous
    Abstraction—and the attendant
force and pity and accuracy—
with the individual you see
    drinking coffee, daydreaming, bent

on buying a belt or handbag,
    breaking up with their girlfriend or
choosing to answer question nine
on the essay list for Design
    and Society, say, or sort

sadly through their mail today, or
    hum a tune. I realize that
these theories understand me—
explain, and hold me—just as cruelly
    as they do any other, that

they do so more probably—though
    I don't see it as 'cruel'—that
lack of exact fit a kind of
supplement for the human. Does
    this suggest some space left that

'makes room for' the *soul*, the mad vibe
    that keeps the motor ticking? It's
a rhetoric I can't stand. I
just want to have my thoughts, not
    understand them. Does this

make sense? Nope. "The Cone of Silence",
    a phrase I've learned from friends younger
than me, fans of Maxwell Smart—though
is my usage correct? I know
    The Way-Back Machine (of Doctor

Peabody's), I know Gilligan,
    I remember Maynard and "Work!?"
exclaimed with shock and surprise. I
never really approved the tie
    Steve, say, felt, to the afternoon world

that colonized his brain, or Adam's (?)
    though they're common currency now
between Crab and me. The Way-Back
Machine—something this poem has
    become, inadvertantly. Now

"My heart, in the tenderness of
    Friendship"—in Johnson's phrase—wishes
to address itself to Julie,
Mikey and Chris and be solely
    in the present—*or Rome*, with its

busier streets, strong coffee and
    entirely interesting (because
foreign) surfaces, feel and past
that will be new to us. Rome 'starts'
    in two weeks—we'll live a few floors

up, in an old building, in Trast-
    evere, the studio of
Malcolm Fraser's sister and B.
R. Whiting, *not* watering the
    plants growing on the balcony hung

above the street—though I hope to
      stand on it mornings and dusk
and watch the street and skies. Though is
this reasonable—maybe there is
      no view—or space to stand? A brusque

knocking on the door, I gather,
      announced an officious *poliz-*
iotto (the dictionary
gives a term that is maybe
      better, considering, which is

vigile urbano): he'd come
      to reprove one previous tenant
for causing water to drop on
the heads of those below—his own
      one imagines. Urban vigilant,

caped crusader eyeing testily
      some geraniums and—out-of-
focus—white wrought-iron railing . . .
and tile and slate roof, miles of it—
      or am I thinking Paris? (Doves,

maybe a church tower or dome.
      I will see when I get there. The
tower suggests Northern religion,
whether Catholic or Protestant,
      and where the Italian dome

says Belief the dark, grim spires
    of the British-style churches I know
suggest threat and mostly drear
failure to comfort.) I've no idea
    what we'll find. *No* view. Maybe no

geraniums. But sky, and clouds—
    those heavy shutters that close to
keep the sun out. I loved them when
I was there before—July and
    fairly fierce sun. In Adelaide who

has not put up with far worse, liked
    it even? I loved the nondescript
street we stayed in, briefly, the first
time in Pisa. Admittedly I used
    to love the view of Rundle Street . . .

from my office window at night—
    a neon light said *Rossini's*,
another said *Prudential*. We used
joke about a wise, even *ju-*
    dicial drink that beckoned via these

red and blue lights in the dark night
    and amid softly lit doorways,
windows, and parked cars. In daylight
I loved it too. Supposed to write
    from there I did manage. The change

of scenery might do the trick
    again. Change and stability—
in this case writing might be the
stability—and Cath's presence.
    Repeatedly, I see Julie

across a table from me, in
    Rome, excited, curious, her
head turning, focused on the flow
around us. Mikey and Chris, both,
    would fit in smoothly—more Southern

in appearance, though each bearing
    their British surnames—Grimm, Chapman.
Like Julie I look anything but
Italian, she Anglo, my mug
    Irish, I gather, and foreign—

plainly—in dress, stance; Australian
    by virtue of diet and weather.
Cath's lovely dial delicately
Irish and refined—fluently
    speaking Italian I hope: her

brain our forward defence. Her French
    is great. For me six months as a
Cigar-Store Indian, standing in
silence, behind, beside. The words spin
    by too quickly. "Cigar-Store Indian"

an objectionable phrase, as
      well as obsolete: do they still
exist? Better *Il Cono di*
Silencio. Could I seem
      'Bohemian International'?—

Maybe, with Cath nearby. I should
      encourage her to pack her most
raffish clothes. Funny, to be training
for Rome at *The Flash*, where being
      Australian has—almost

as often as 'being modern'—
      been my main preoccupation.
One's life resembling an oyster's:
breathing in, breathing out what is
      close to hand—a meditation

on (duh) Time, and History, Style—and
      Subjectivity—from *The Flash*!
Basically, a guy who reads a lot
is reading, having a think:—What
      Is going on here? A brief clash

of traffic noises, cups, voices—the
      sudden pathos, beauty, truth-to-
type of some passing figure, the
recurrence of the familiar,
      a change of the light—the girl who

looks like Julie—just barely—here
    recalls Catherine Demonget—
was she the oddly dream-like one,
in *Zazie In The Metro*?—one
    is plunged into deeper thought, a

sudden empathy for someone's
    imagined situation. IS
THIS JUST 'THE COFFEE' ?! Intellectual—
without-portfolio we call
    poets. Every day, oyster-like: sift;

sift. Though to me it seems human.
    If inefficient.

Long Distance Information

Dear Crab,
It would be great
to be drinking with you, here
—because
There Are So Many Bars
& walking
between one & the next is
terrific at night.
Rome
resembles a beautiful film set:
mysterious, melancholy, & hip,
hip & corny existing
side by side
—but the corny is them,
not you, so you don't have to worry—& the hip
you can
emulate
or blend with—& you'd be *up* to it.

I keep intending to write :
remarks mostly,
all trivial.
Otherwise we're travelling
—*this* place was nice,
that one wasn't—sort of thing.

What goes on in Adelaide?
Are you busy? Playing music
much?

Working on things?

The travelling—

Pisa,
Florence, Bologna, Venice

with Anna
(each
for just a few days)
Terracina
then down to Lecce
—the South—
Cath & me;
to give
a small reading
part
of a conference, that consisted mainly
of dinners, lunches & parties
enormous Germans
walking into plate glass doors
& rebounding sobered
A 'Greci' band
earnestly representing
their remnant culture
(a 14th century survival of Greek settlement)
&
The Beautiful People
(some)
& arties, hipsters
local aristos
or 'notable families'

#

So, seen a lot of historical art
—the Baroque in Lecce is
'something else'
In both senses
I.e., not Baroque—& *way out*.

I've become
slightly interested /
in Italian painting, of the 20s to 50s,
very melancholy & dispirited
I used to just think it was hopeless
—hardly having looked—
now I like it

Bought some CDs by Jimmy Scott
—popular
in the 40s & 50s, with
'sophisticated black audiences'—
one of bad 'live' recordings
& another from 1999.
His voice is amazing—it never broke
really
due to a rare medical condition—
but his style is mannered.
It sounds like Nancy Wilson (as I remember her, from the sixties—
though it was *she* listened to *him*)
& he sings Bryan Ferry &
Mick Hucknall ballads,
'Jealous Guy' & things.
A mistake
to buy them probably.

No music here.   I sing 'Down in Black
Bottom' a lot,   some Fats Waller,
Johnny Littlejohn, Howlin'
Wolf   —
& whistle a bit of bop.
Hey, our tape from
Supermild
's disappeared. Hold on to yours & I'll copy it.

Strega is a great drink.
This I have found.
Though $3
at the Bar San Calisto
buys about 5 inches of it. Almost enough
to lay you out.

And as I drink less & less these days
& don't have much
to say
it is the walking about,   the setting down,   the
first
taste
& the getting up, gladdened,
everything rendered
alcoholically greater
I dream about.

The Italians themselves
don't drink a great amount

or not to excess

& to stumble about

slightly crocked
would make you feel boorish
a foreigner
most specifically one who had willingly
declared
himself
alien
& therefore uncouth
rude at any rate
which the Italians
don't warrant

John Forbes's notes to this place

—all past residents at the studio leave tips, advice—

include a theory for
Why Italian rock music's *no good*
Which goes
Italian kids are too well loved to feel alienated
& to go & sulk in their garages with the amps turned up

&, similarly,
they don't experience the same need for oblivion

Italian pubs
exist
—mostly calling themselves *Madigan's*
Molloy's
or *True British Pub*
(like their teas—*Sir Winston's*
Sir Andrews, *Sherwood*) —
but the Italian kids

don't stagger from them /
ripped.
We lived a few days above one in Lecce.
Each night
closing time resembled Adelaide's—young people
standing about outside
a few sitting—daringly, in
la maniera inglese—
on doorsteps.
In 15 minutes
they were all gone
—no fights, no shouts, no crying

Little cuties.

So, come to Italy & go on the wagon!

Though, curiously,
I saw two beggars
(who *seemed* drunk)
complementing each
other
symmetrically
sprawled more or less identically
at opposite sides of the Oviesse steps
(a kind of
upmarket, down-scaled Target)
calling out to people.
They looked
as if they'd been lifted from somewhere like
the corner of
Raphael's

School of Athens

Of course, they seemed happier
—*if* 'philosophic'—

though I doubt if they'd been drinking *Strega*

Anyway, people, old ladies,
Took No Notice, *used*
the stairs to Oviesse
to get in & out
—the babble of voices
not suddenly hushed, in
fear or embarrassment.
Where
the Oviesse is
seems very French to me: that is,
it doesn't,
but I can't work it out—
why doesn't it?

The 'French' thing
is the plane trees
that are pollarded
so each tree is like
an inside-out umbrella,
pretty leafless still,
branches ecstatically
imploring the sky,
looking
any of 'celebratory',
'austere', 'calm', 'awaiting'.
Their trunks

are pale grey
& speckled; the sky
—thru & behind them—
looks bright & silver
& far away
& sort of serenely unpitying,

or blue
& quietly Fauve.

I guess it *is* Italian
after all
—as well as Parisian—
& in Paris the buildings
might be uniformly taller,
coloured more neutrally
no yellows, no reds
—more Citroens & Mercedes ?

It is somehow a little less thinly 'sharp' than the French feel
more mellow, less sad

Enough of this. I love it. You
would too.
Stendhal says, in his *Guide*,
how ashamed he is
to have announced an instant love
of Rome
It is a commonplace & he's embarrassed

&,

as he wrote the thing without even being here, you have
Every Right To The Same Opinion!

(By some logic.)

The Logic . . .

of the Strega!

Time for me to whistle bop a bit

collect my
'thoughts'—

or let some more home in,
the head resembling a kind of
dove-cot.

(I'm reading an older poet, whom I'll
probably meet in the
next few weeks
—poems about Death,

held in abeyance,
by his ironic manner
framed, *triangulated*,
via
high-cultural props
—the Renaissance, the Baroque
Brahms, Mozart & Wagner—

but, then, *he chose to live in England . . .*)
Speaking of warriors

(were we? did we?)

& music
(we did)

the bus shelters here
all have pix
of Lazio soccer stars,
photographed
as if they're
centurions
or gladiators
—one looks like Little Stevie
of the Easybeats.

Another thing you'd like: the back page
of Rome's *Yellow Pages*
—it goes by that name
maybe
internationally?—is one big ad
for a Telly Savalas-looking
guy
who's a Private Detective

Tony Ponzi

bald head,
dark glasses,
collar of his trench coat pulled up

"The certainty of knowing everything. Always," it says.
"Resolve your personal problems. (Beware of others using
similar name.)"

There must be competition.

Seems to handle divorces, industrial
espionage, everything.

Anyway, I may tear it
off the phone book
for you.
(Should you *need* a detective he operates
I note, *"in tutto il mondo"*

So do I, tho strictly via
airmail

Tiepolo

In the 14, 15th &
16th centuries it was
all happening in Italy
artistically tho by the 17th
other countries had joined in.
By the 18th
Italy was definitely off the pace.
Still, I happen to think Tiepolo
was a major artist
tho employed mostly
by palace owners
to fill space—
before the invention in our own time
of the smoke machine
that so readily solved this problem—
for disco proprietors, rave
parties etcetera. In the last week of
third year old Bernard
pulled out all the stops
in the lecture on Tiepolo. I was there.
Not alone, but almost.
(Others were at home, preparing
for exams, finishing
last, overdue essays.) Like Professor Smith's
lecture that no one heard
Tiepolo was designed
not to be looked at.
Like the smoke the machine
pumps out: billowing cloud

. . . some armour . . . flesh &
garments—the suggestion of
excitement—that no one buys—
least of all
the lonely type,
who can't dance
& stands, staring into
a corner
at a trick of the light.
Tiepolo's *Three Angels Appearing*
To Abraham in the Venice Accademia
is like that. He is the dud guy
bottom left—kneeling, dirty feet,
beard. The angels, thin limbed,
glamorous, surf up
on their rubber dinghy of cloud—
& look down incuriously—
except to remark, perhaps,
the dirt—& vouschafe a glimpse of
beauty—a limb dangled
Abe's way, silhouetted against cloud.
As if to say,
You can go home now,
Abe, patron-at-disco, better not
to wait for more.
You've been catered for—
it costs a lot,
but they've got everything here.
Here today, gone tomorrow.

Which doesn't solve your problem.
Ciao!

Rumori

> Down in the windy park the leaves all turn
> over at the same time—it's the climate
> explaining the weather to the workers
> —'The Romans', John Tranter

> A problem, that, solved, would render one almost
> no longer Australian.
> —*The Bias That Makes The Ball Roll*, Ervin Thomas

out the window rises the hill,
with the houses of the rich people. Apartments.
The view—unusually after a month in Rome of
good weather—overcast.

Lively, bustling Rome—where there is plenty of the past, definitely,
though where, for me, ghosts of my own country's past
approach & murmur & back away
as if,
having taken their number on entering the room,
they queue & file, waiting to be processed—imagery I think
that comes from Nadezhda Mandelstam—& my own experience

of buying a lamp at the electrical store—
Vorrei una lampada:
men—builders, handymen, electricians—

standing about in overalls & caps & parkas
to buy the fittings, yards of wiring
they would need.

Destinies. Aspiration. Ideas
more or less capitalized—Romantic & abstract.
And the pathos of 'the human'.

For me,
always, cities suggest these things. So that
to visit them
brings these questions up.

Though I never answer. And they return each time
familiar, with additional features, histories of their own—*their* history

of my not dealing with them.
(Though "dealing" suggests some finality.
Which will never come.) Merely, "these are the things that I think about".

("Ken, your friends are here."

Oh-oh. And they walk into the room—
Christopher Brennan, Slessor, Grace Crowley:
suits & coats & mufflers, a paper bag with alcohol in it.

A flat I visited very young a few times—
Connie, a friend of my mother's—down
steep steps, it looked out through trees to the harbour.

Cremorne . . . Mosman. The characteristic Sydney trees & flowers,
the tremulous fifties

—a kind of
Adrian Feint view, out a window.
A small wicker table. I wonder how accurate

all this is.
                    The thematic fifties personalities—
thirties & forties—imagined entirely, though I've seen
photos of Slessor.)

*

I shut the windows to the apartment.

A famous painting by Boccioni, that I love—
because I love the idea I suppose, but also

its domestic & feminized form in the picture—
is *Street Noises Invade The Apartment*:
a woman (mother, wife)

leans over a balcony or window sill
& all the activities of the street
'penetrate'—through the walls, through her & the opening.

It was an embarrassingly large number of years (decades?)
before it finally twigged for me
that where it said on the slide, or reproduction,

"rumori", the word did not mean "rumours"
(or "suggestions") but "noises". Futurism:
so deadly—*or* loveably—clunky

in its 'execution' of ideas.

But they *are* like rumours—hints, ghostly

callings—the noises from the street here.
Shutting the windows reduces them to a rumbling, pleasant
background. I will open them again later. The view

reminds instantly of the densely housed rise
up Kings Cross from Wolloomooloo.
(From somebody's
flat you saw that—Sal's old place? an architect's office I visited?
The same view
you saw more distantly from the Art Gallery.)
Or—
a Sydney city beach suburb's view. Bondi. But the Trastevere
area is more built up, the styles more various—

'30s' thru to now, the ornamentation more particular. What else?
White features less often. A huge
salmon pink number is dominant on the left. Otherwise

tans & yellows, some shades of orange—stepped & ranked
down to street level—where you peer down from our patio:
at *Station Pizza*, small shops, garden walls. Trees occur

at more frequent intervals than in the equivalent view in Sydney
& a different sort—tall dark pines, cypresses (which must
always *spell* 'Italy'), olives &, more surprisingly, wild,

exuberant-looking palm trees. Our first morning
I was particularly struck by the closest palm, that grows
near an angled junction of roads opening out

onto the main road beneath. The tree fills & overflows
its space. So 'twenties' it reminds me

of a Roy de Maistre painting—that I assume exists.

(Am I thinking of a flower piece, or a quite different view?)

I decide it will make a drawing—in
my mind's eye I can see it looking like
de Maistre, Kirchner, Matisse—& also Brett Whitely.

(Though how, if I'm going to do it?)

How will it look, when it's done?
The hill overall reminds me of Grace Crowley
Her picture called ... *The Italian Girl*? Probably not.

Tuscan Landscape, maybe—but a hill
of similarly graded cubist planes.
Cath comes home, has a sandwich, cup of tea

& goes to bed—to nap & read—before
we visit Pietro, our 'third Italian'. We have at last begun
to make contacts here—after days & days

of adventurous walking—along the Tiber
& into town—through ruins & monasteries & parks & villas
Vespas, ambulances.

"Goethe's Foreboding," the latest
TLS is headed. I've scarcely read him—& should.
The picture one has—a cross between Mme Recamier
& Oscar Wilde. *Rising to the occasion of his picturing*,

all that is on his mind. *Not* foreboding. He
worried about The Poet's Place In Society. Or his
own? At the Protestant Cemetery, despite

the signs that promise it. we fail to find him.
We find Gramsci.

*

The tree's exuberant,
20s feel—via the association with de Maistre—
& the immediate identification of the hill opposite

with the Cross, usher in this same group of thoughts
I have often in Sydney—as
a 'foreigner', particularly. That is, I never had them

when I lived there. Though maybe it is Time—
these things would have come to me 'eventually', & did, have.
From Sal's newer flat, from Laurie's, they have

swelled romantically, like heavy weather, banked
clouds over the headlands: the intense, romantic blue
of the harbour—yachts, boats even, being

'of the past'. Sydney—1938? '46? '52?
At Coogee at Michael & Di's I list these themes, the list
surfaces from time to time—lost eventually.

Ideas mocked & evoked by a sight one time at Kurt's—

As they are mocked & evoked, as it happens,
in Kurt's thinking. (Do we all think this? shuffle
these same cards?)

'Sydney'—a group of images—that says 'Nix' to dreams.

Yet the elements—its beauty—encourage them.
Hence the town's pagan & hard-bitten quality. Which I read
as acceptance of failure. Like the falling back of the waves.

Slessor. The failure of its artists (their names
all minor). And, like any city, it suggests the aspirations & failure
of capital 'c' Civilization—& of its politicians, by whom we mark the years
(Gorton:

deposed as party leader—

"And what are you going to do now, Prime Minister?" "Go home
& watch *Countdown* like everybody else." Keating,
Hawke, their various bitternesses): highrise Development

& the Unknown Past . . . —the beer ads of the 30s & 40s—
that decorated, once, all the pubs. Preposterously,
men in suits; women in formal wear, bare shouldered;

waiters, aspidistras, smokes;
the long-necked bottles of the beer itself
memories of my father.
It all proves nothing,
it seems to say—though, individually, each piece

says something else—like the surf's tumult
ending in a hiss, as it fails to take the beach.
Like the leaves that turn over in another's poem.

I visited Kurt one day—&, leaving,
on my way down the steps, the vertiginous view
between buildings showed—quite close—the intent figure

of a bodysurfer, deep brown, frowning—in the grip
of the moment's exhilaration—bright flecks of light bouncing
off the blue. 'Life'. These aren't questions exactly.

Undivided pleasure—small, yet it looms.
Perspectives that are incompatible. Is it this pathos
Sydney is about? or Australia? Me, merely? A

life as if *writ in biro* (more modern, more
sensible than water?) My new pants,

surely more sensible than Goethe's. Though
like me he may have found his get up
eminently suitable, in Rome—& been less wrong in this than me, too

—though he'll have paid more—all that white silk—
& been right of course, about so much else beside.

The intent bodysurfer—
what does it mean: *I should swim more often?*
Things look great but they're *not?*—

yet surely better they look that way
than worse? Or is that the trap

that suckers you—for 'this unhelpful binary':
Bernard Smith after a lecture—
chin rising defiantly.

*

Like a sore you regularly finger, an ache you press—
these notions, this 'idea' of Sydney: clouds gathering dramatically
out to sea, rolling in—(me, moved & conscious of it, thinking

Why did I leave? Will I come back? What have I ever
made happen?) On the house high up, on the right,
on the verandah, grows a cypress that has exactly the hunched

brooding shape of the Böcklin figure I know from
de Chirico & Klinger. It sulks or worries there
every day, arms folded, chin on its chest, comic, inconsolable,

a dark presence. The 1880s, subjective, German view
of Italy—its olive green melancholy, its quiet, its liquid stillness,
& depth. Or something. Cath says today, looking up from

whatever she is reading, It's Goethe's son, not
the man himself, we should have found at the cemetery.
Odd, then, the signs proclaiming 'Goethe's Grave This Way'.

We joke about
The Lost Sock, an imagined series of Klinger engravings.
We've lost one, at the laundry.

There's the sock thrown in the corner of the room—
there, alone, in the clothes dryer—a dog trots down an alley,
a crow flys off—with the sock.
                                        Once, friends had thought
Klinger was the German in *Hogan's Heroes*
& that the old reviewer, Elwyn Lynn, was being unusually hip,
to mention him, in connection with their work—in which clothes
were eerily depicted.

                                        Hip, but differently.

The first few days in Rome I feel myself
turning into an 18th century Englishman,
a plump guy in breeches & short frock coat—with a tear

in his eye—bits of Rome looking so sub-Claudian:
ruin; medieval addition; a stand of trees—needing only a shepherd
to admit that, yes, it is the Picturesque, or stage machinery.

Hard to have an attitude to it that seems modern—*without
ignoring it*. Which I don't want to do. I zip
into town & find the central post office—a square

that always turns up about when I'm about to give up on
finding it—& post our letters (Anna's, Cath's,
mine) & go off to rendezvous with them at the library—

our impressions of Rome winging home to Adelaide.

Time to do that drawing.

*

Ideas that are no Big Theme. That pose no question.
Just ‘the way I see things’.

Olsen
is not so minor. Tuckson isn’t. Grace
Cossington Smith’s drawing—
of men going on strike, a protest, a rally—I like.

And the loss of heart & confidence in the twenties—
the deaths, the small
place afforded, after the War, in the wider world

our volunteers signed us up for—

that diffidence, caution, disappointment
get built in, built around & built upon
become character. Which makes me just the frown, the

slight stammer Australia bears into the coming aeon,
a kind of polishing of the glasses—what is the gesture?
a chewed lip? a narrowed mouth? Whatever—

& whether true or not—I like this view of things:
iron taken into the soul—which strengthens,
like the small dose of poison. If nothing matters,

nothing matters then. It is all
"in the face of negativity": Tuckson, Guston, Pollock . . .
Grace Crowley—whose work I love, more than Kandinsky's—

for the contingent reason: its tentativeness registers so much of this.

*

A puzzle you pick up & put down, & walk away from.

Small objects on a table—a marble, an ashtray, a postcard view.

A shelf of books beneath the window.

*

Amusingly, the students we read to
remark the next day *how 'humble' we were*
—which we explain as national style. The Italian guy

who read after, introduced his poems at considerable length
giving them, probably, *strong recommendation*—then read them
with *a lot of feeling*, seemingly surprised at how good they were.

The students were nice.

And Rome is great—walking aimlessly through it
as it is lit up tonight, all of it is beautiful, much
resembling a film set—Rome in the 60s, actresses, models

sportscars, fountains—light picking out the textures
of walls, greenery thrusting from stone & brick, streetlights
bright & fluorescent—and a constant randomness

to the flow & sound: darkness, quiet,
then sudden flaring of headlights
(Vespas, voices, bodies emerging from a doorway—

& entering a car, parked at such an angle & in such a way,
that joining the traffic now streaming past will be an effort—
an adventure, *and* achievement—but won't mean running *me* down, thanks).

The road I'm on rises before me, peaks, disappears,
& appears again higher, further away. Phosphorescent,
silver white, the streetlights strung beside it like pearls

rise & dip too. I am reminded of Melbourne
—though which part—& Sickert & Whistler—& Clarice Beckett!
that same sad eye: a vision that strikes me as 'teenage'

not because it is inaccurate or to be bettered: that is the age
at which it becomes available—an intensely sad & stoical projection.
I think of Laurie as I write this. —'Mr Melbourne'

(though others are thought to be—& want to be—or are
only that & seem diminished . . .). His letter today.
I wonder
do I have Clarice Beckett's 'eye'? "Oh-oh, a lonely

teen-age-er"—lines from a song John Forbes used often remind me of.
—*Why Must I Be A Teenager In Love?* (Another.)
John was Sydney. As is Pam. *For Love Alone*—doesn't that have

descriptions of Sydney I always meant to read? Where
can I get that book in Rome? I am somewhere, now,
near Via Dell' Umilita & Via Del Corso, & undecided—

not between those things though—humility & business.
I'm for business. At least, I think, tonight I am.
I go home, call the drawing finished—spray it with fixative.

It looks okay. A bit of Rome, a bit of Sydney—
perhaps London a bit. 'The London Years of
Roy de Maistre'—a Sydney remembered.

A Sunderland appears & lands whitely in the harbour,
a corsage. I think of frangipani & carnations,
look out the dark window—at a Rome that isn't visible—

& see
the hill, the variegated pink & cream houses, verandahs.

*

A puzzle you pick up & put down, & walk away from. A rebus.
Flaws in the glass by which to see. I replace them, this constellation,
small objects on a table—a marble, an ashtray, a postcard view,

a 1960s beer coaster. Items that
mean nothing—though they make up
'a sentimental picture of Australia'.

A perspective—distant from Europe—that lets you see
more accurately than they do, do things
with less assurance—but do them anyhow,

amused to be making the gestures that are art
with all those gestures claim, or make them
with no claims. In fact, the coordinates I love.

As someone, somewhere in Rome, a Roman, must be
making a painting, making a poem, knowing Rome
is not a centre any more, that Italy is not central.

Yet they go on, happy, thoughtful,
Rome's night air outside the window, spelling *Rome*.
Many happy hours, Pard.

Holden Song—or, Homesickness Was His Middle Name

> Here, plastic furniture seems like a good idea,
> more natural on a marble chip
> & concrete terrace, as though
> what we treat as objects,
> they take for granted
>
> (hence 'style'
> and how for us this word belongs in ads
> —'Roman Poem', John Forbes

Reading about Marie Henri Beyle
I suddenly wonder if Murray Bail hasn't named
himself
after Stendhal—Marie Beyle. Why shouldn't he
of course, despite . . . Or are the similarities numerous?
Anyway, an act of faith. Cath, Michael, & Di
have gone down to the markets.
I, in an act of enlightened disbelief—
after all I have been before—
remain & quietly read
&, now, inside, write—
another act of faith. As the trams
roll by & traffic noises—horns mostly,
but distant ones—bleat & sigh, complain,
or mechanically & pleasantly
drag the moments by. From where I sit I see,
outside, the white plastic chairs
John was so caustic about, momentarily, in his poem—
& beyond them, six feet further—green shrub
& the pink-&-biscuit-coloured facetted climb
of buildings on the hill opposite: warm, calm, marked by
the grey-white *horizontals* of verandahs—

the *vertical* accents of window frames, aerials,
&, dominant, one dark green pine.
Above, blue sky, & a bit of awning hanging down
                outside our doorway,
the door I look out to see all this.
John joked severely
that the plastic chairs that, to us,
would look less than ideal
or even cheap, at home in Adelaide
in Rome look sensible, approaching elegance, & closes
with those Australian expatriates
looking fondly on them, turning
their hearts against Australia.

My point? None, as usual.
Two months to go, of our stay here in Rome—
where the chairs look okay, to me,
though, true, I wouldn't like them
at home—where
I can't wait to go
though happy for the time to run out
at its own pace—
where the sight of the first aged Holden
will make me smile—like the thought
"Murray Holden Bail."

A Prospect of the Young KB as a Critic

"For a long time I stayed in bed very late."
—Marcel Proust

I remember with a kind of spiritual / intellectual
'wince' the boredom of the papers on Sunday. The comics.
The last page, if you still hoped
for some relief (it was, after all, 'the last page'), featured Val
(Prince Valiant), Radish, Laredo Crocket & maybe
The Potts . . . (& some puzzles, Chucklers, I never did).

Radish I remember with some affection. Though did
I feel it then? Rarely. In it a couple—or a threesome?—engaged in
        intellectual
problems thought to typify their late-middle-aged, maybe
almost 'battler' status. There was no action in these comics—
& in this instance, invariably, the old lady, her hair worn (like Val
's) in a bun (Val sported, when I think about it, a curious Cleopatra cut),
        dried a dish or waved an admonishing finger—& hoped

or worried that—say—money, which she hoped
would arrive, *would arrive*—& pay their bills. The bloke, though he
        did
hardly anything (& nothing that didn't go wrong)—read the paper, bottled
        beer—or carried *his* device, a manly hammer—tightened a val-
ve that needed loosening—& while he talked over his shoulder she
        wiped up & talked back. (As fair to call this "intellectual"
as "abstract", I think.) *Maybe it would happen*, maybe it wouldn't,
        whatever *'it'* was & one rarely knew. In these comics
long-foreshadowed action—maybe

because it took so long & was uneventful—like tension 'going away'
rather than definitively ending—did not *seem* like action, & maybe
Radish held some microscopic fascination—how I think of it now—
because, in a pasture out the window he grazed, the 'wild' or
trump card we hoped
might one day be played—in a rescue of narrativity, surreal but
consequential. *Radish*, the last of the comics
on this last page, took its name from the badly drawn, sway-backed
horse—suspended *leit motif*, incendiary loose-cannon narrative
device—available, should its creators feel (as I did)
the need for it. In fact weeks would go by in which we did not catch
sight of the beast—& then we did—leading his contemplative
(not to say intellectual)
life, truly a Life of Riley, munching, chewing, raising his tail. Was he
their unconscious? their libido? The Potts' *id*? "Val,"

Prince Valiant's flaxen-haired betrothed would say, "Val,
stick it to me." But she never did—though she admired him, as I never
could, while he practised his archery, sharpened his sword,
'had moods'. Was this maybe
muscular Christianity *avant la lettre*? or a puritan paganism? Val
never promised the violently insurrectionary the way Radish
did, or even the intellectual
far-fetchedness & 'possibility' of the horse—who had a rumoured
history as a one-time winner: hopes hoped
of him had some basis. Val on the other hand, had done nothing—text-
book stuff, dutifully, text-book battles, text-book dispensing of
justice, text-book falconry. There was no melodrama. Val did
everything in orderly fashion. He would never even grow bored with
himself, bored enough to come bursting through the door, cigar in
his mouth, gun in improbable hoof, announcing *He-haww! The
Drinks are on me*, as the horse would ... or would in the comics

I desired. Was the strip named after the horse, as I imagined? Then who
were The Potts? Or *Wally & the Major*? Why, of the comics
on the other page, was the one I understood least the most intriguing—
the modern one, temporal miles from Val
but geographic miles from me (I assumed it was America, though almost
too literate—which made it, then, socio-economic miles from
me, too)? where what they did
was *sit*, & amble around, in an airy open-planned lounge or den—&
maybe
read the comix, or Sunday papers or a magazine. The heroine hoped
she would not be bored, & father—handsome, quizzical, sporty
dresser—made dry remarks—as did mom—another intellectual?

The young girl (eighteen? twenty-two?) wore Prince Val's hair-do,
better than Val did,
& torreador pants & maybe lounged on her spine, oblique & petulant—&
hoped
her boredom would end: like me she hated the comics . . . & Sundays . . . an
attractive young bourgeoise—while I remained, *like Radish
before me*, a 'dark horse'—yet, like the girl, soon to grow
fiercely intellectual.

Ju-Ju

Wayne Shorter when
you don't need
him to
be great
  is good
when you
need help
  is no use

which I think is maybe
A Definition of Cool—

a gift & congratulations—
to your good mood.

                    Coltrane
is more reliable
& is Great
but is never cool. I would
buy *both* your music
a drink.
          Yes,
tonight *yours*
Wayne too

Amaze Your Friends

I watch an old Errol Flynn movie
Custer
The last half
—Terrible reception—
What nobility
Then the last third or quarter
of an old
French movie
beautiful & rivetting
a
Simplicity
that is almost humorous, if you
Contrast it with modern films
—soundtrack
Of rustling, & a lone bell

& the beautiful,
Intent teenager
moves with deliberation through it

Before it ends
Anna, our teenager, comes home
A little like Mouchette the film's heroine
soaked
& moving deliberately
but happier than
the actress—
Nadine Nortier's character
Then
I pull out an LP

I haven't played for a while
to fill the end of
A tape I'm making
& the tracks *Devil's Island*
Moon of Manakoora, *Black Orpheus*
are great
Did Wayne Shorter ever do anything better?
well,
The stuff with Miles equals it
—*Dolores, Freedom Jazz*
Dance
Gingerbread Man—
but by *Island* & *Moon* I'm made
As happy as music has ever made me.
Earlier,
Tonight,
singing an old song my father used to sing
& thinking of him
has maybe set me up
For this untroubled ascent of spirit
Banana
Takes herself off to bed
last night she refused
& fell asleep on the couch
wouldn't wake to rise
I watched a bit of *Rage*   there beside her, her
Blissed out body
lit by the TV screen. It was
hosted
This night by Tex 'Whoever'
From *The Cruel Sea*
Who showed old clips—mostly it seemed for reasons
Of physical deformity or abnormality

Mick Jagger's
Big lips
singing *Girl With The Far-Away Eyes*
very funny
& my heart warms to him too,
his send-up of Gomer Pyle
His dial prettier than, but resembling, Barney Fife's
a girl
with
Very big tits
is the stated reason for the next clip
as tho
To say "I know this is an odd reason
but wait till
you *see* them!"
Then Iggy Pop working *very hard*
To an entirely unresponsive *Countdown* audience
of
The young
who fail to wave their arms, scream, *or*
smile even—
Tex's point. Well, I try to wake Anna
again
Decide she's warm enough where she is
& go to bed.
The
Needle lifts off
from the vinyl, a second time.

I play it again.

A friend's poem once commented on
his bladder's being

his metrical device
—he was writing in a pub—
something
I have almost never done
—or never to good effect—
The needle lifting tho
I've experienced that
Sudden attention
drawn
To the relative quiet
& to some aspect of your concentration
A gentle sound.

Moon of Manakoora
Written by Alfred E. Newman
the father of Randy Newman, &

Whose name featured on all those film credits
—late night & midday movies I watched
as a kid—
& *for that same reason* apparently
chosen
For *Mad Magazine*
that irritating lunk-head
who was their logo
What Me Worry?
What
a culture!
Well, I'm in it, & of it
Thinking just today, at the gym,
where Bruce
Springsteen was playing

—unusually : usually
it's disco, hip-hop—
What better confirmation of Adorno's
point

—the masochistic use of music's repetition.
Songs sad, & to *be* loved . . .
& *Born In The USA*—an anthem
red-necks cheer for, on American Wrestling—
to honor
their boy

& chant identification

yet the song means to point
To disillusion.

Know yourself I guess. I'm
Too serene tonight
to want to think that thru
to
any diminishing conclusion.
My father went before
me
& had, maybe, all these notions
in t-shirt & shorts
On the back steps, in
the kitchen, down the bush
that started beyond our yard
They are
their own reward
point to the fact of the time
& freedom to have them
— brief.

Hindley Street Today, With a View of Michael Grimm

What to do
          when the day's heavy heart,
                              settled,
                                   rises then—
thru some quality of the light—
                         & you your own mug
                                   raise up
                                   to see it,
register it
          bing!
                         the way counter staff would
                                   gain change
in the old days,
          but not any more—
                         & not 'today', today
being *now*
          (& in *this* 'day & age')—
                              Those old-time cash registers
                                   having gone
before *the electric typewriter*, even, disappeared
                                   —tho
                                   I never
                                   had one
                                   of those.
          Why,
               pause, & reflect, & look down the street
where Michael Grimm might come
                         —& with any luck holding
                                   in his hand

the tape you requested
& he was pleased to deliver
notionally.

Tho ‘notionally’
Notionally might well mean “Never”
Have you got it? Well
give it here!
Maybe he does.
On it several versions of *Bauhaus*:
“Bela
Lugosi’s
Dead”.
It’s too bright & clear
in Hindley Street—
for him to be about,
the Count.
Yet, the waitress says—
“Yeah, I frighten a lot of people,”
says jokingly
tho without much effort
as she clears the table
where I sit today
outside
to a patron whom she’d startled
—& actually, tho she’s
pretty enough
her makeup’s vaguely ‘Goth’.

I find her interesting
—as I look up today
& down the street

looking for it to confirm my intimation
& expanded heart
With a view of, say, seraphic Michael Grimm
& my tape
on which
Bela Lugosi's dead
studio version & 'live'.
He's dead
& Dion
& so is Bing.
Bob Hope lives on, I think,
tho barely
but I'm alive
& Michael & Julie & Chris—
& those dead-heads from
the Arts Department
they've moved in
& now they find *us* 'more alive'—
we
laugh
at that,
'good naturedly',
the street is cleaner, too
since
they arrived
a reason why
the light strikes things better now
&, if this coffee haint improved
my mood has
as I think, Yep
—of Michael,
The Grimster—

will he have done it yet?
Too soon.
"Too Soon"
—the Nirvana story
it usually is
too soon, I guess
even Lugosi might have thought
One more day,   a week!
I think, "not yet"
I've got
the 'Hindley Street' template out & operating again, the
details falling in
—'signed up' for the long ride,
Tho less some days than others
but
just this minute I'm up for it.
The street looks grey & white
& muted
benign *—or* tired— or
more forgiving
Is that just the lack of traffic?
Temporary.   And the lull between the late
breakfasters
& the early-lunch crowd, the time
given
the waitress to talk
the old men
at their tables, plotting
—plotting nothing—
the Tech teachers at elevenses, me,
& fucking
Michael Grimm — the
nut

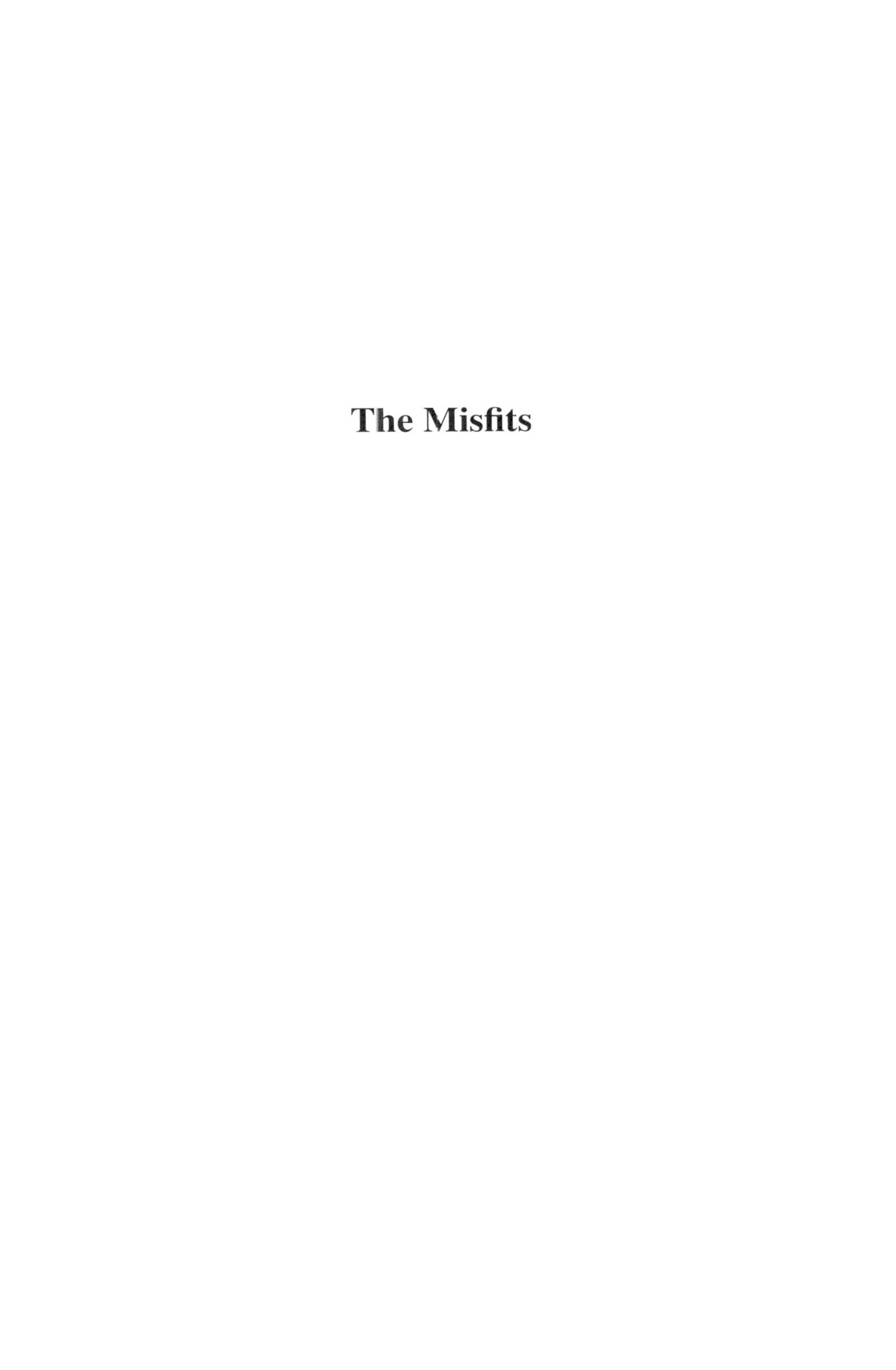

The Misfits

Coffee

1
there are a number of things I always liked about coffee

2
drinking coffee alone I can enjoy reading Tony Towle
much more, or who*ever* I like

3
one of the things I like most to do
is drink it standing at my door.
which leads out of the kitchen of our flat
& faces on the tin of the fence
3 feet away. above the tin
is the view. it is the city—something
else I like.

4
drinking coffee out of a small cup which I like I enjoy
thinking about a problem of contemporary poetry: *too many
poets* like the word "blue".
I myself like it. —the sky
is that colour
& in the distance, against it,
the tallest buildings of the city are against it
or reach up into it cool-ly. Some cranes near some of them
do it too

5
My coffee is finished

& I am lost in thought, leaning in the
open door.
the cat & I
are getting on quietly together.

which is
no big deal. —neither of us wants to 'live' in

'The HAIKU'.

6
the sky / is looking all
blue & 'oracular'. hours before
a huge cloud was 'choiring' there, like a New Realist's version
of Tiepolo. both of them
tell me nothing. (that is, the sky being *blank & clear*,
& the cloud) the cat seems unaffected too.
I feel the way I hope Robert Motherwell might feel
—pagan, & immensely cultivated.

7
as so often happens when I drink
coffee alone I don't think of anyone but myself

8
the coffee has a bitter taste I turn my head to the left
as I change the foot I'm standing on
& down the path is the view between the two white, modern flats
of the water a narrow but terrific

strip of it.
I feel terrific myself. The wind—
which is moving it & making it
look like it is living is touching me. I like this particular contact
with the air &, indirectly, with the water—
looking 'elemental' &
deep blue between the buildings
—like Anthony Quinn
in the Mediterranean being
clichéd

9
I see him on a Greek isle in a little bayside
cafe, in the open 'Life' is bustling around, & even though
he has to do
something important, he drinks his
small coffee
& says—of the coffee—"It is good"
& it is, it's terrific, coffee.

Good Friday at the EAF

weekends here
are the best: beautiful, quiet
I sit in Caron's & my chair
the one we share, at the desk
between our desks, the shutters
letting in light
all is white, the shadows
diffuse—multisourced—
light coming from many directions
I'm beginning to die myself I see
because mostly I sense I cannot see
too well—& have almost a headache. Julie
types way across the space on the computer
the rustle of language that quiet rattle
Michael came in, adjusted some
of the new equipment, & left—dressed for
tennis. Julie is dressed
differently too—
tight pants. Only I am dressed
the same—
but I am dying. And it is
Good Friday. Big deal, it will
take a while
I make tea, get paper,
start this

How I'm Feeling

"a relaxed Carol Linley"—Bill Berkson

The 24th of November!

+

And yet, *despite* that
"artists must never weep" (-Beethoven)

+

The orange day of the poem
rages on, still!

+

The Actors !

"a relaxed Carol Lynley"
a favourite line

+

Ben Gazzara (well numb my stunning mind!)
doggedly talentless bore! Studied
Creep!
movie-wrecking
Ben Gazzara

+

Great to be a poet,
great to be a painter!
Great to have some cigarettes!

+

CRAB IS JUST A SOFTIE !

+

& I don't even smoke

+

see the way I do this, a little
state-of-the-arty ?

+

my heart sets out
on another one of its trips

+

"Carry my beer while I weep!" "Is there
                a Tissue in this pub ?!!"

+

Rundle Street,

where I sit (outside)
in the cold night, lovely
& clear, & think about this girl, Deborah.

+

woman.

+

aeolian heart—aeolian mind

+

You think I'm Romantic ?!
But *I* know what **You** think !

+

a small
poem, of obscure encouragement

+

what to do with it ?

+

In respect of Zen though: "That way
lies Madness"

+

too unsung (?)
on the contrary—
not unsung enough !

+

"Nope! I don't have *'a thought*
in my head'!"—George Brent
his characteristic expression. (If it
could speak.)

+

would you of

+

The cat butts my chin with its own little head
—a head butter for love!

+

I'm not on any porch—that's
Tony Towle (poet), Cole
Porter, or *some*one

+

sex

+

I guess I will win out

+

This doesn't 'mean' anything—I hate poetry
where it does, don't you?

+

One 'looks back'
—from the railing you're always
standing at, say,
to inside—the lit room,
the desk, the carpet,
the curtains long & white
emotional

+

I said it cause you'd like it

+

Driving home I figure I 'get thru
the traffic' *by* Logic of
Strange Position

+

Maybe you will 'get' to like me.

+

"The dopey effect of the third person"

another great line. I agree with.

(By Stephen Rodefer)

+

& here is another one—which proves it.
"he was about the only decent conventional poet around, as
far as he could see."

& "The FBI
seize all Iran's de Koonings."

+

Would you think less of me if
"with my biro in my mouth, sand drifting over my feet"
I *thought* this ?

–

&
"how are you feeling / in ancient September?"

Poem (The Ice in my Glass)

the ice in my glass goes crink!
as it adjusts to the tequila—keying in
that sophistication—the feel of it—I associate
with these tall buildings—a bit of the
skyline of New York I envisage,
important to me for many years—

or if they weren't, the buildings stood
for the idea of importance, New York—
an imaginary number filling out
an order—of which the others were a part:
the finite Melbourne, Sydney, Glebe—
& Fitzroy & Bega. *Did* I think about it?

But it became less important—& then, almost by accident,

I visited, & saw it—specific, real—
& loveable, surely—if less impressive than the
rarely summoned abstraction. Strange—
& terrible—to think of it threatened,
New Yorkers frightened—as the city's image
draws retaliation upon it. Clink, the ice again, settling.

My New York—the notional one—the city of poets,
of art. I met one poet there—'perfect'—
urbane, bohemian a little, worldly, smart,
immensely intelligent. (The art, there, was in galleries
& historical—great, but not like the poet.) My
second time I met rich people—the sort the terrorists

think of: people congratulating themselves on
the world & their ownership of it—talking deals, leverage,
new fields, salaries & investment. We were on a penthouse roof
near the UN building, looking out over the water
(towards New Jersey?—somewhere) for
the fireworks of July the 4th. The same UN building

as in James Schuyler's poem, that moves slightly—in
the wind, the light—or has that building been torn down & gone
& this is a new one?
                    The New York I like—
personalized, romantic—about which I know a great deal,
detail—things that have happened there, what one poet said
to another (at Gem Spa, at the Morgan Library), the

books they read, thoughts they had: unreal again—
a fabled, picturesque locality, of thirty years ago.
A little like the Sydney I now visit, which I left
in the 80s & in fact *hardly know*—can scarce reconcile
with the site of my former life there: where X said A to Y,
where 'L' lay (or sat) & wrote 'Sleeping in the Dining Room',

or 'A' began, "Saussure! Saussure!"—where I lived, round the corner
behind the Max Factor Building. I didn't meet the rich—
tho Sydney has them—resembling New York's probably
& voting just as vociferously
to support war on the Afghans.
Frank O'Hara, a hero of mine—a one-time hero, a hero still—

mixed with the rich a little. But as was said in his defence once

recently, he never owned more than two suits. He was not of them.
I don't like the Sydney rich—for wishing to be interchangeable
with their New York counterparts. Which is *as I fancy them.*
Tho as it said on the Max Factor building below the name—
"Sydney London Paris Rome New York"—& I aspired
in my own way, too.

Funny, all the papers have pointed out
the Auden poem, "1939", has been much quoted—
& some Yeats? Would Rome or Berlin—Paris even—
have sent minds to poetry? It is the enormity of the act—
New York as symbol—& as never attacked before.
I wonder if it *is* a new era? You'll read about it elsewhere—
not here. If it is. I might look up that Schuyler poem, "Funny

the UN building moved / & in all the years / I've
lived here" or something—or find the O'Hara one
in which he stays up late trying to select his poems
thinking, good or bad, he *did* it at least. Wrote them.

Now
I've found out what I think. Very little.
As I might have guessed. An event moving 'under the skin'

away from words—& become attitude.

Events
will be bigger than me. Having ideas about them being
almost irrelevant. Though I 'have' them: none helpful or
resolvable: that the New York I liked, even then, came
at a price, that *today* does, & that I don't pay it.
The free ride you complain about—would you get off?

As usual the exchange rate dominates the news again
—a cargo cult
The dues you pay are servitude—so you can hate yourself,
or wonder merely at the duration of the ride

Some Thinking

Does all art aspire to the condition
of music?—While someone

is always prepared to say so I put on
a tape, a CD, *instead* of writing

or put it on to write to.
As far as the art gets.

A tape rolls quietly—"Light Blue",
"Soul Eyes"—to which I've done

a lot of reading, a lot
of pottering about, a few drawings—

& to which I've 'cleaned house'—

& a lot of writing—or of 'trying to write',
which comes to the same thing. Mal Waldron

wrote both these tunes.
                                        I came across him
first in the poem for Billie Holiday—"The Day

Lady Died", with the great last lines
where she whispers to him across the keyboard—

"& everyone & I stopped breathing."
The great thing

about the line is the uncertainty: is it "everyone
& *I* stopped breathing"? or that Holiday whispers the song

"to Mal Waldron & everyone"—& it is *then* O'Hara
"stopped breathing"?

It makes for a pause, a hesitation, a number of them—
that evokes the magic & tension

of her timing. And there's Frank, leaning there
—near the door to the toilets? The 'john',

which always suggests the hard American 50s—
& ensures I think of him in a white shirt & narrow tie,

suited. Already the texture of life is disappearing
—exactly how it felt, to be in those suits, in that time, at a nightclub

how anxious or not, how preoccupied & with what—
how people held themselves—is gone. Well,

it survives somehow, unverifiably, hard to quantify,
in poetry . . . we still have the music, films—

but films lie. Cassavetes suggests the era to me—
was he 'the type' of the hipster—cool, up tight, hip, witty?

suited, a drinker, free, & maybe more exploratory—
within limits more circumscribed than now?

Or do we always see ourselves as more free—
& get it wrong? Did he

& O'Hara meet ever?
Different worlds.

The thing I was going to say about nightclubs
was that maybe how people feel & act in them

never changes. (I heard some magical things
at Lark & Tina's, for example. I've been as tense

as anyone, at the Cargo Club—& wore suits there.)
But night clubs themselves might've changed—with the music:

amplified is different? the fashion for recorded
dance music, or for dee-jays, might have altered them.

On tape one of the moments I like best is the voice—
a little shakey, a little spaced—Jim Carroll's by repute,

asking for tuinols, in the space between songs, at a great
Patti Smith gig. Or Velvet Underground—

they're both on that tape. There's some great
& wonderfully casual, relaxed things said, over the music

at a late 50's date that features Miles Davis
guesting with local hero Jimmy Forrest: a type of music, & experience,

continuous with the live recordings of Charlie Parker—
the same carefree ambience & same reason to pay attention

whereas Patti's music gets to you pretty much
whether you listen or not. You don't have to choose of course.

"Jesus died for somebody's sins but not mine"
is always great to hear said. This track,

the badly named
"Soul Eyes"

(how can you not roll it
into one word?), is not live but so sad & so unhurried

it makes *time*, development, almost its subject. John
Coltrane. Well within his limits—*as*

somehow imagined—& great the way conservative paintings
by great artists often are—a Gauguin still-life

that looks as though it wants to be Manet, or Fantin-Latour.

Roman Friends

—for Pam and Jane, in an apartment I once occupied, in Rome

Roman Letters

headed straight for the Pantheon, the Colosseum & such
—Pam Brown, a letter

ah Sweeny Todd
will we ever forget "Him"?'
—John Forbes & Mark O'Connor, 'Admonitions'

what time is it
in Adelaide   in Brisbane ?
it's after 4 in the afternoon here
—Pam Brown, in Rome, 'Early October'

The end of Winter—Spring almost. I sit here
in calm, cheerful Mandarin House. Sunday. A beer
I ordered on its way. (*Did* I order it?)
Are *you* drinking beer, or drinking wine—
as you swelter thru Rome's record heat? Mid
day? midnight? Still so hot, I take it, you both
watch television—French, not the Italian—loath
to hit the street till dark. Here the grape vine

out the back has greened, almond blossoms dot
the lawn—*are still on the branch!* (I wonder what
the weather is like over there.) It will soon not
be cold enough to wear the coat I bought
in Rome. We arrived in the cold—hot
when we left. The green here surely means there
Autumn should begin. Is that how it works? Where's
room service? Who made this? The maker ought

to have left instructions. (*God*, some ancient
said, *is very small, quite minute*—an ancient
I love for saying that.) God, a bell-hop, sticks
his head around the door—Italian—ready,
seemingly, to serve. Or Spanish? According to his
press, Julio Iglesias was *"the Spaniard
Most like God"*—Is Ricky Martin now that Spaniard . . .
Most like 'Him'?—Another 'locution' that heady

poem 'Admonitions' taught me to like (to speak
of John, who got there before us. Ha ha. He'd
have agreed swiftly of course about *getting there
before us.* I mean Rome, where it seemed odd
for him to be—tho John seemed odd everywhere
he was. His poems suggested he found it odd too,
or depressing. His having found it so
made it easier for me . . . given something

to think about.) . . . This factotum 'god', about two
foot tall, resembling Ricky Martin—resembling, too,
Soutine's red-costumed bell-hop—grins and disappears.
("Runs off giggling" . . . "sniggering into his hand"
—from Ron Padgett's 'Wonderful Things'. Every few years
I read it again and am moved.) Pam, my first memories
of Rome include walking up that hill of roofs and trees
opposite, that you sent photos of, taken where you stand

on the balcony and look across. It was cold.
A family trudged on before us. We stole
up on them, young mum and dad, tiny daughter's
hand in theirs, talking, complaining, steam-puff clouds
as they breathed. Behind them walked the

son, five or six years old—dressed like his sister:
luxuriantly—well-tailored coat, shoes, muffler—
cute, miniature, singing as he walked along, not loud

but clear, resigned, and happy, lost in his world.
After a time the magic of the song turned
everyone's mood—theirs, ours (foreigners, unbeknownst
to them, a few yards back)—into a calmed
transfiguring moment. Nearly every time I walked
that hill at dusk that memory returned.
I hope he is happy still. Though what a stupid
thought, or 'useless'. In a few years, newly armed

with a Vespa, he will rupture the silence
everywhere, like all Italian youth, bent
on love or dollars or honour, drugs or debt.
(Oh, save him, save him!) Anyway, when it cools
maybe you will make that walk. Dusk, remember. Let
me know what you think of the houses there.
Some were beautiful. Middle class, an ideal—where
Testaccio is more communal in feel,

public. Did I mean 'idyll' earlier: the
solicitous, caring, proper, proprietory,
well-turned-out amenity and deference
well-heeled Italy projects? Like the kids'
beautiful clothing. I did, finally, order this
beer. And now it's come. Southwark Premium
The Chinese waitress asks Is it 'South Wark'?
An old English word I tell her worn down with use,

'Suthuck'. I am wearing the coat, enjoy it—

warm *and* elegant—for six weeks of each year. It
is my 'Roman' coat. Rome sounds great. It's so cold
here today that I love the *idea*—of Rome, and TIME—
(the 'element' not the magazine). I've told
people on occasion that I dislike heat, that heat
affects me more than many others—
but *my idea of heat* . . . has *no* effect.

The Colosseum seemed an evil sort of place
to me: brutish. You knew as you came to face
the steps inside that it was just 'Rugby League',
but worse: it had a callous, hideously male
feel to it. I get the same feeling in many pubs—
threat and danger. Being a sensitive sort of guy.
Have you gone to Celio Montana yet (Sky
Mountain—can that be what it means? It *was* a hill)

or to the parklands I recommend in Bakowski's
book of tips? (Hmm. And is it cooling?)

#

Laurie won the *Age* Poetry Prize. He'll
have told you I imagine. I'm happy for heem.
Some duds made the short list. But don't they always?
Laurie said with the money he'd buy a sofa.
Which made me think instantly of Andy Capp.
Remember how he used often to be lying on it,
fully dressed, back to the reader, knees pulled up,
dozing, his cap still on? Not exactly Laurie.

Probably not entirely unlike, either.

Cath's away for a week, visiting our 'property'
on Bruny Island. I haven't been yet and have only seen
photos. It's the only place we could afford land,
but it might be nicer than a mere investment:
Cath thinks it's beautiful! So you two can
holiday there some time if you want. Tho you'll miss
the Baroque after Rome. Or would you? There's Robert Dessaix,
if you're looking for something over-wrought—and Richard

Flanagan—is he realist or gothic? This last week—in
my standard reaction to looming deadlines—I've been reading
The Balcony of Europe, by Aidan Higgins.
A book that used to be remaindered
—in the 70s—all over Sydney. The first 50 pages
were beautiful. Then it turns into the sort of book
you love when you're twenty two: worldly-wise
bohemian love affair stuff: a bit like *The Sun Also Rises*

but with no dramatic action and lots more learning,
and the author just elaborates on the female mystique
for a couple of hundred pages. (Philosophical drooling.)
Nicely written apart from the tics that help it pretend
to knowledge and gravitas: verbless sentences
announcing, apropos of nothing, *facts* . . .
of history or biology or animal husbandry,
or asides or observations on national characteristics

and on the nature of man and woman—and lots of phrases
in foreign tongues, for the Romance and Beauty
that they just *have*, dammit, just have. (In italics,
so after a while your eye learns to skip.)
Terribly sophisticated about Jewishness, too.

Patronising about the whole Mediterranean.
It's better than much of what I *was* impressed by in my twenties!
But now . . . sort of amusing, sort of tiresome,

sort of funny. And, stylistically, the agenda
of every sentence amusingly obvious.

I've been MC-ing the EAF talk series
(The Modern Nonsense) for the month
that will end next week (Sept 4th).
God they've been the sort of thing
that make you want to gnash your teeth.
I've got to try to make them look good,
help with questions, etc. We let this one
be put together by an outsider. Big mistake.
He left town, so I had to handle it anyway.

And it has largely been idiot academics, who couldn't
say something simply if they tried or who wouldn't
in any case—complacently opaque,
querulously inane. Much better when we had
artists trying to explain their last year's activity
with a few slides. If I strangle a speaker
at next week's talk, of course, *then* I'd be in custody
and wouldn't really be expected to deliver the lectures

or go to the stupid reading I'm down for—two lectures
and a long catalogue essay—all due Friday-thru-to-
Monday, of the week after next,
the week of the reading.
It's an idea. I'll write to you from my cell,
if that's how it turns out.

By way of a poem I send *you* some stuff, too.
I liked yours by the way. Tho I left the *print-out*—
of letter and poems—at work, where it's supposed
to remind me to steal SOME time from mere
processing of new titles, ordering of more books.
I read them over morning coffee middle of last week.

Of course the poems I'm sending you . . .
only so-so.

Romans, Two

> Last weekend in Abruzzo was great. We walked up an impossibly
> high-looking peak—rocky & piled up, bare and peaky . . . with
> a small stone chapel & bell tower on one of the peaks
>
> Jane & I at the Terme di Caracalla both in bad moods, wondering,
> as usual, why we were here but feeling obliged to look at more
> ancient brickwork just because we ARE here—& so *we should be
> grateful*. That's the nutshell really. Eat your tripe, you should be
> grateful ! . . . and I LOATHE obligation.
> Maybe I should follow some of my Rome studio predecessors and
> just get drunk?
>
> —Pam Brown, letters

Hi Pam. I keep wanting to do these things
as a poem. So I'm way behind, meaning
the poems'll be arriving—addressing *you* in
Rome—long after you're back in Sydney—and you
will feel they address someone *in
no way bound* to answer them, 'as letters'.
Not that I intend this rarefication, emptying of ethics—
but with so much to say about Rome, so much to

remember even, this way is fun.
Maybe I could write poems (like any ordinary person)
at least *without* the rhyme scheme—and so stay up to date
(if I can't write straight *letters* like anyone else)?
I've liked YOUR letters—your poems too. Make
Laurie send you his 'September Song'—if that's
what he's calling it still: in it he places us
exactly where we are—him on sofa, you in Rome, bells

ringing—and me, precisely, at the Baci.
Very precise—tho the Baci's name's changed. (Are we
aligned correctly now? For the record, October 1st,
2003. Three-thirty in Brisbane—so he might be on the couch.)
I've begun this second epistle. A short burst—
not so much of energy as of will:
an exhausting half hour over my lunch-time coffee—till
I've eked out these three or four stanzas. *Not much*—

when I've been 'worrying', for a month, that these letters
are not the ones you need or are not *when* they're
needed—arriving late, infrequent—and as if you were
a mere pretext for a poem. In fact
I think if I keep 'remembering Rome' in this manner
it will probably seem to you not *your* Rome—and
oddly distant, and beside the point—when
I could be communicating something that

you might want to know or could be plausibly thought
to want to hear . . . what's happening, what I think. (Torched
cars out the back we never witnessed, no. We had
a horror month of enormously loud and continuous
drilling in the flat below, the building mad—

all looking daggers at the renovators, and at the apartment's closed
door.
Our floor shook and vibrated from eight to three—poor
Cath I remember lying staring at the ceiling, nerves just

frayed till three came round, too ill to move. It was
hot—late April, early May?) Old Trastevere, because
it felt so much ceded to the Anglo-American
tourist, I never entirely liked. It felt unreal,
too beautiful, too seedy, too glamorous and
like a privilege unearned and not to be enjoyed.
I mean, I liked it but I liked it best devoid
of people—early mornings. The stage-set feel,

then, was beautiful—the narrow alleys, varying
rooflines, shuttered windows letting the cool air in.
Is one unselfconscious, at last, or unambivalent
merely—not conscious of divided opinion,
thinking one thing: *it is beautiful?* Trastevere—where,
later, it will be crowded with the rich and would-be louche—
the tall blond waster sprawled beside his eurotrash
friend, and sign with hand-written inscription—

Help me feed my dog—and the dog of course. The sign
not even written in Italian—feckless blithe
spirit? An idiot?—or is the passing trade
more receptive? Is it less desperate, more
romantic, in English? The Italians regard
animals with less automatic sentiment. *Cane*,
the pitiless Latin. *Mondo Cane*. Only
half an hour these last few lines, Pam, or

did I start later than I thought? A process poem
with a rhyme scheme! A diagram,
as I joked to Laurie, of the penny dropping!
(As opposed to Whalen's 'a graph of the mind moving').
Thirty years ago I laughed aloud, coughing,
writing it down—the slice in the lecture, *Dog
and the World* by Franz Marc, a truly risible, dud
painting. The dog looked like Pluto. (There's an amusing

painting like it—in spirit—by Alex Katz.)
The dog resembled the one in *Blondie*—that's
if there *is* a dog in the *Dagwood* cartoons?
I might be remembering John Wesley's slightly
pornographic but amusing variations on them. Tune in
to my mind and this is what you get—an endless
reel of jump-cut images. Does anyone care—about Wesley, Katz?
(I don't mean to run them down.) Is this why I read

all the time, so as not to attend or analyse?
Dog in the World, anyway, was the bald translation, idealized
in the German (*Welt*—what's 'dog' in German, *hund*?). Spat out
in Italian, it's an estimate of rank, not the fond
Anglo-Teuton extension of fellow feeling. The Walt
Disney aspect of the sign's appeal (the happy
share of it that 'goes' to the Huck Finn Dane
or barefoot Pommy, sitting beside bowl and sign and dog)

makes me instantly, stonily, bitter—too horrible,
too false, on too many counts. The artificial
aspect of tourist Italy produces this reflux effect—
in me—the not so very sensitive tourist.
Italians must find it tiresome. But is it

reasonable for me to bear their burden—
embarrassed on their behalf? for the
world!? Perhaps the hippy was embarrassed too, as

he cashed his bowl of coins in—for *chinotto*—
and some larger denomination notes, no
doubt—or paid off the tab wherever his lunch-time
pizza came from. Where was I? Apoplectic, like
Stendhal—far more an Italophile than I am
(I mean, more reasonably called so)—that least coherent
of men. Someone said that of him. In incoherence
he might have met his match—*C'est moi, Beyle!* Yike,

this leaves me ten minutes to get the mail
and get to work. (Exits restaurant Beyle-style—
grim, frowning, man of action, of the boulevards, of 'town')
A quick Hi to the waitress and I zip down the street
whistling a jaunty air—incisive, insouciant—that I have down
pat and must concentrate to identify—
of Junior Wells's, *Everything's Gonna Be Alright.*
Did I really make that joke to Laurie?—at least

I meant to, but maybe it came to me after—
after I'd emailed some remarks about his 'September'
poem: the thing that would make it me
rather than him would be to add the connecting
"who" and "which" throughout so each new phrase seemed
tacked on, an extension and afterthought, "diagram
of the penny dropping". Laurie's relative compression
reflecting his more distinguished mind—or my mind's slumming

to see the syntax do its purl and plain, concepts linked

like carriages of a train. Sam Cooke's *Having A Party*
linked the phrases together the same way—well, not similarly—
but endlessly, and in a way I loved, the end of the sentence
forever deferred. The things *I* mean to say
get endlessly deferred. A favourite memory
of Rome—a kind of first moment we
knew we were going to be alright, first moment

of elation, of tension disappeared: Cath had
just bought new shoes—Techno Crockers—we
loved the name—mustard, pumpkin-yellow sneakers,
solving her footwear problem. We were walking
along Lungotevere ("beside the Tiber")
towards Testaccio. Cath began to march happily
taking big stamping strides, swinging her arms
exaggeratedly, stepping long and high, smiling at me.

Rome! This was great. Suddenly
I was happy too. The value of larking around.
The long curved sweep of the river where the Lungotevere
follows it round from the Aventino to Testaccio, the Tevere
flowing brown and placid. When Spring kicked in
it became turbulent and powerful, dragging small trees
that snagged against its bridges, lapping close to the walkways
down by its side. The big, modern bridge that carried traffic

from Testaccio to Trastevere—where so often
we saw accidents, motorcyclists lying still,
as police and ambulance attended. We walked there
to the cemetery, to the markets (fish and shoes,
I remember—but, now I recall, vegetables, too)—
and to restaurants, to our friend Silvia's. The housing

largely from the twenties and thirties: large buildings built around
square internal courtyards, beautifully shady and quiet,
an aged working class hanging onto them, now much sought after.
In these first days we hardly knew 'anywhere'.

I think Cath wore a large, rust-red, tunic-styled jumper,
crocheted. The image I retain: her smile, her eyes,
the reassurance and encouragement—the 'lighten-up' button
pressed. We both began to sing.
Testaccio was the other neighbouring area
I walked lots late at night—to Santa Sabina,
to the Circus Maximus (often beautiful at dusk,
always great at night, so huge, so empty, so run-down,
so atmospherically lit—the dramatic ruins across from it—

the scale: always distantly tiny bunches of people—kids—
having an illicit smoke, a couple embracing, someone walking
their dog, some desultory fooling with a soccer ball,
teenage girls gossiping—and emptiness:
always an air of the furtive, the secret, the illicit,
the futile. The park lights lit up this enormous expanse
of green—a lozenge-shape in the city night—so that
its atmosphere seemed tangible, like the dome of a water-world/

snow-world thing—miniaturized, but also reminding
of a past Rome where the space might have been used
for goats, cattle, and cooking fires . . .
and painted by Lorrain or Rosa . . . or Richard Wilson?).
We made four good friends, Pietro and Marlene and
Alessandro and Pesach. Pietro and Marlene
I associate with magic—miraculous cooking;
a tiny flat on the roof of a high residential tower,

as confined inside as a submarine's quarters; the quickening
view outside, of the city—train yards, bridges,
buildings, river, the tendril-like furze of aerials, antennae,
on all the roofs, delicate against the rose of

sunset and the descending dark—the whole world
laid out, small, below—lights incandescent pearls
of white, or the softer, fruitier, duller crimsons, blues,
oranges of fluoro signs—and the magic of Pietro's
students' performances in *Bluebeard*, ex-students who'd
returned each year to star in his productions
they were so good, as good as I had seen
in professional shows at home—the main roles

at least. They returned to the tiny apartment too,
to drink and smoke and be enthused and test their ideas,
endorsed by Pietro and Marlene so kind—
the most beautiful young woman that year in the feisty
female role and two very funny guys. We were there.
It was a joy to be drinking, laughing, and talking
on their roof: the chill air, the great view, the city's
noise filtering gently up—distant traffic, sirens,

the clank of shunting trains—the young people's faces
full of charm, verve, and enormous good-humour, and,
though sophisticated, unmarked. Italy's high unemployment,
the dispiriting dependence all young people had
on family—the threatening half-life enforced this way—
stood before them, incredibly. They came regularly
to visit Pietro and Marlene, for encouragement, and as
friends. Alessandro and Pesach were in their thirties

(older in Alessandro's case), and working.
Adult lives, ringed about, as any life is—but underway.
Whereas Pietro appeared (magically) *by chance*, just when he was
needed—speaking English, offering to translate my need
to send and receive a fax, then telling us to call and meet
for lunch—Alessandro and Pesach *had been recommended to us*—
by a Melbourne friend. They were intellectuals, more or less,
two gay guys, teaching and writing, working in media. We had

a number of very pleasant times with them and their friends.

Briefly we were part of Italian life, of *some* Italian's life, not
tourists, not outside. A life, though, that seems to propel younger
people into a kind of early middle age and embourgeoisement:
(young couples seriously examining sheets and kitchen-ware).
(Shouldn't they be dancing, drunk, or playing sport?)
Whereas here, everything predicated increasingly on youth
and youth 'culture', middle-aged Australians are left feeling
life is over, that they have *no* culture—except that of being
out-of-date, irrelevant, unfashionable. I wonder if this is

true? I remember being in the would-be bo-ho San
Callisto Bar, where Italians who aspired to living
outside these bounds sometimes showed, along with
the slumming tourists and the undoubted artist or two
(I suppose, though I don't know). A guy came running in
one morning, yelled *Hey*, grabbed his friend's tie
and blew his nose on it loudly. All pretend. It struck me
as very funny, uninhibited. The bar was deliberately—

or complacently—seedy: run-down old kitchen chairs and
formica tables inside, peeling cream wall paper, plumbing and

air-duct pipes blossoming largely in the oddest spots,
odd photos of old boxers and sports teams on the walls—
the service hilariously brusque and terse. They served me the
largest, most deathly slug of Strega one night.
I was drunk before I got to the bottom of the glass.
Outside one morning, I saw a young guy, around thirty,

sitting, with his baby in a pram or pusher. We were sitting in
the sun, me reading the *Guardian*, probably—at one of the bent,
unbalanced metal tables. He was terribly nervy, shaking—
no, not shaking: his foot kept tapping and he chain-smoked.
It was as though he was not used to this domestic duty
or pastime. The child's mother should be doing it. But what
should *he* be doing? Drinking coffee somewhere with some
other guys? Writing a poem? Reading? Clearly he was

unemployed, merely and simply—but without the ostensible
justificatory prospects, even that of *choosing*
'the good life'. Not working was all that was available.
It was not a choice. Well, who can choose it in Australia?
And how rosy or secure are *my* circumstances? I am
not sure what I am saying. But it was something Italian
I witnessed, whatever I made of it. He pushed the pram
back and forth with his hand as he sat, a few inches

either way, without pause. Open shirt, curly hair, foot tapping.
I should write you a real letter, Pam—so you don't feel
cut off? Though 'cut off'—that's the best part about
being over there. It is, as you say, a kind of enforced rest—
almost boring some days. It'll all be over too soon.
(But then, I'm never ready for the obvious—never ready
for 'even' the obvious.) While this guy was quietly fuming,

or dying for a drug, I was importantly engaged on
my enforced holiday, trying not to feel every minute self-conscious.

So, that 'real' letter:

the Abruzzi sounded beautiful. We considered getting there,
but we never did—time constraints, funds, and worry
that we wouldn't find a place to stay. I like the idea
of the torched cars behind the flat. I'd forgotten
the janitor's wife Chiara's name. She was a sweetie—
but she took against us, a little, after we'd given a bottle
to Antonio. Once his hangover cleared, tho, *he* was a lot friendlier.

Romans, Three

you and Laurie make me feel
like Shelley vis a vis Byron—'a glow-worm
to your mighty sun(s)'

I have seen the San Callisto. I didn't go in.

Hi Pam and Jane,

I have just read your latest email letter—
written on return from Barcelona, Espana.
And my responses have jostled themselves
into the order of their importance or urgency.
(I always find this experience funny and need to quell
the simultaneous disheartening: the
'blurted-out' quality has to be
tempered somehow. I mean, in a letter. It's

okay as immediate email reply.
But as a letter it seems unmannerly—
coming in an ostensibly more considered form.)
The Byron-Shelley comparison:
I wouldn't worry about it—and probably you don't:
tho *I* do, thinking my stuff has become
diffuse over the years, as yours has hardened, become
more economic, and sharp, and telling.

(Laurie moves between the two extremes—
without resembling either of us too much. Well,
at least we can be told apart.) (I first
saw fireflies in Italy—Piazza al Sercchio,
near Lucca: are they the same as glow-worms,
the glow-worms Shelley compared himself to?
The latest Complete Shelley, I read just yesterday,
has dropped one of my favourites—"Evening:

Ponte al Mare, Pisa". Apparently it was
a 'fragment'—that Mary had chosen for the Selections
made after he died—partly to demonstrate that he *was*
'immediate' and 'responsive', not just an
anarchist ranter. A pretty complete 'fragment'
in my view.) Your letters have been great to receive.
Of course, you're *supposed* to be experiencing the place—
you can 'write it up' when you return. I didn't

write a lot while in Rome either. And, anyway,
these anxieties (the sun vs firefly thing)
are usual and permanent. I'm sure
you can live with yours, pursuing the pointed apercus
and implied overview—while I rattle on (as John Tranter

once remarked of some fool, “like a froth machine”)
feeling I’m being . . . what? Audenly? Byronic? Derek
Mahony?—basically, passing time. The thing

I felt most tho was the wish I had visited the spots
you prefer to mine. I will have to get the map out—
to see if I didn’t in fact go there. I hope I will be able
to feel I *did*—if you can work that one out.
The street names are familiar, and the landmark churches—
so I know the area. The San Callisto, granted,
was in some ways a silly place—and maybe possible
only in the conditions I was bemoaning, I don’t know.

But after a point one wanted *some*where to sit down
without having to reorientate yourself.
I reckon you should go, tho—and have a nighttime Strega.
Jane can help you home.
I wonder how you’ll find
Bologna—handsome, but a little treeless
was my view, but tho I covered a small part of it
fairly energetically a few times over,
I didn’t get a firm handle on it, even a firm

wrong handle. Everyone comes to Venice
prepared—so many old hands and old views of it,
and Venice confirms them all or seems to vouch for them.
On a bad day the endorsed Venices seem, on the
evidence, imaginable. (I saw it but didn’t love it,
tho I sometimes forget I didn’t, it was so memorable
and full of great art. —Tintoretto!) Modena? Is it a car city—
where is it? I’m sure I associated it

with racing-cars as a kid. North, I suppose. I'll check.
Well, you can expect I'll try to turn this
all into a poem, Pam. (Easy—set wide margins,
right?) One of the places you went to with
Eileen I sort of know—Via dei Genovese:
we got lost there repeatedly in the first few weeks
(and also between the Tiber and Botteghe Oscure)
and didn't go back much till the last month, tho my

hairdresser was down there (Via di San Michele or
San M di Cappella, I'm not sure which now—
she used to cut Jean Shrimpton's hair! Actually,
"style it", she was careful to qualify, not "cut"). It was
so cool and quiet. The other place I think I *don't* know:
Porta Settimiano I can't find. It'll have to stay 'yours'.
Hope the lift was working when you returned! The wall-
paper in that lift always reminded me of

souls-in-hell. "Los perditos!" I once tried,
when squeezed in there with a native—who
looked at me askance (my bad Italian? bad
Spanish? or tempting fate?—I don't know. My
bad hair, maybe. I've just had a haircut, Pam,
a week ago: I don't look too bad—and 'normal': that's
the big payoff, though I'll gradually become
'that weirdo' again . . . in the coffee-shop

writing to Rome.

Love,
Ken

(Pinkham)

—for Gregory O'Brien

I wonder how
Gregory does this
these three line

stanzas & whether *I*
can do them—
to any good effect.

I make coffee, check
various things around
the kitchen—find

the new clock
I got Gabe for his
birthday, note the

milk is almost
gone, bring the tea back
& sit at this finely red-&-

white checked table cloth
again, pick some rice off it
from the meal tonight

chew it, & start—which means,
mostly, I stop here
& see how I've done

It has my characteristic choppy
          rhythms, etcetera. Oh well.
                    It is called after

Albert Pinkham Ryder
          —Gregory's poem—
                    "called after" an American

phrase, that I guess
          comes to mind
                    as I recall

what little I know
          of the American artist—
                    19th century? or

very early 20th?
          I visualize small
                    emblematic paintings

typically
          with a dark image
                    centered—briefly

silhouetted—
          against a dark background—
                    a sort of horse-&-rider

against a storm? (The image
          my mind remembers
                    may even be

some late sketch by Moreau
        —you know: the late,
                atypical unfinished

heavily impasto
        fragments that
                art historians love to suggest

the Fauves might have seen—
        miles from the
                stillness, & detail,

of *Oedipus & the Sphinx*
        say—or “in most ways”
                Anyway this is miles

from Ryder. And I am
        briefly sure
                it is Ryder I can imagine

& the Moreau too—*his*
        horse & rider
                in reds & blues

lemon yellow, the American’s
        black & deeply
                varnished colours—browns—

against a discoloured
        white, or cream
                & a larger dark ground.

Tho who knows?

Ryder
is not really our business

a reverberation of US
culture: local news
like CNN, the

American breakfast program
we get at night. What a
hopeless analogy. Ryder is better.

Moreau—
well, I like to bear in mind
his presence

along with Manet &
that revolution. Tho
give me Manet

any day, if I had
to choose. Tho, um, you don't.
I like the portrait

—full face, almost filling
the frame—of Moreau
in a bowler hat

high collar, & tie, narrow
moustache—very
1900s modern

by Roualt (pupil
    & friend) that is
        slightly 'cubist':

the one eye furthest from us
    —it is three-quarter on—& that
        whole plane, of cheek

& wide wide forehead,
    swells out, flattens,
        just slightly.

It seems an irony
    of history—
        or perhaps the irony

was Roualt's. It was
    mine too eventually
        (though less originally)

when I did a copy
    of it . . .
        that I liked

& seem to have lost now
    Misplaced. I haven't seen it
        for a while

(I could do it
    again.) I take the rest
        of the tea

& toss it on the
pot-plant, beneath the goldfish.
The plant had dried out.

The fish wake slightly
& begin to move—
at this angle

a few vague red shapes,
a diaphanous white,
in a tank that looks

dark

Hindley Street Morning with Philip Whalen Quote

So here I am, in the coffee shop,
        with nothing to read but my poem, "Europe"

Nothing to write.
                        "Beguile me with all them blandishments again!"
                                        (Scenes of Life at the Capital)

which I cite on the principle of 'Call A Friend'

    will I lose? will I win?
                            But I finished "Europe" last night—

                        Bits of it take me 'back'
                                        (to Europe)

but most—I have read it so often—
                                                is just
checking out the conformation, the curves,
                            phrasing,
                        how, on the page, it falls or extends

So I sit still, look out the window
                        & some thoughts roll in

all resembling things I've thought & seen before
but I've no objection
                            girls walk past very pleased
to be holding hands with boyfriends
                                        which

seems endearing always
the boys seem happy enough
but
living in a different moment
one just ahead or past

last night I watched *Coffee & Cigarettes*
the Jarmusch movie

—the Iggy / Tom Waits section
not that I liked it best—

Taylor Mead I loved
I watch Rita straighten
the tables outside
today wearing a pink scarf

—I like the way it's tied—

Parisian somehow
I guess it gives just enough warmth
& allows her to wear her usual
black t-shirt & pants
the old guys are all at one
table
near me, inside—
one of them was sick a week ago

but they are all, maybe, there—
unless it was the Ezra Poundy guy
But I've seen him meantime

"Cigarettes & Coffee"
was on my first Otis Redding LP
I loved every track pretty much
I remember its
Amazing clear sound
—Steve Cropper's guitar—
&
arrangements
that were more musicianly, or adult
(how I thought of it then

still do)

than anything I had heard before

having as a teen listened only to pop & pop shading in
to blues

1967? 66? That same year I bought
Paul Butterfield so it must have been 68
& an Otis Spann & Jimmy Cotton LP
one
of the most
beautiful of all

How weird—
I look up
thinking ridiculous to keep talking of old music
this way
& the same girl & boy go by
still hand in hand

Is she counseling him? I wonder—as a joke to myself.

they are both talking. He seems okay—good
mood
nice enough guy
both pretty unprepossessing

he six foot, she five two
in track suits

a guy comes down the street on skateboard

Hindley
is slow enough to manage this safely

still—

Upright, foolish cap on head
he seems
a kind of
visual exclamation mark
something out of a comic

Retro—like *Our Gang, Ginger Meggs*

. . . Norman Rockwell . . .
'Depression era' meets '1960'

10.45
time to hit this on the head
go to work

make a list of tasks for the day

pay bills,
proof the crap I've had to read now
for weeks

(not my own stuff
—drudgery that is *fun*—
'Eaf' stuff)
order books from overseas
(*always* fun)

is My Sarcasm registering here? I mean is it
registering as sarcasm *no matter what*?—I LIKE
ordering from overseas
also: mail-out today

lots of envelopes to fill
some emails from
friends
on the screen
with luck
as soon as I walk in

Notes

- *Home Town*—'Gwendolyn windswept', reference to a poem of John Jenkins' & mine; O'Hara & Towle are New York School poets; Estes & Ruscha are American artists; the *Advertiser*—Adelaide's main newspaper, for which I wrote art reviews for a time; Tubby Justice is a singer, Kertesz an early mid-century photographer, of Paris particularly; August Sander was a German photographer, one of whose works is on the cover of American poet Michael Brownstein's book, *Strange Days Ahead*. Peter Schjeldahl is a New York poet & art critic. The other names are those of friends & artists, at the time mostly in Adelaide: Cath Kenneally, John Jenkins, Laurie Duggan, Paul Hewson, Richard Grayson, Suzie Treister, Aldo Iacobelli, Shaun Kirby, Louise Dauth, Michael Zerman, Mary Christie, Pam Brown.
- *Walking Down From* The Star *Grocery*: Painted blue & white, the Star Grocery—since disappeared—gave Adelaide a country town aspect: an old-fashioned, Greek grocery on the intersection of Hindley & Morphett Streets. The poem echoes a little Frank O'Hara's 'The Day Lady Died'. Yvonne Rainer & Ronald Bladen are American artists. As it turns out, James Schuyler is *not* wearing a leather jacket in the photograph that I was (therefore) misremembering.
- *Halogen Pam*—is, or served as, a letter to Pam Brown, Sydney poet, following on from the earlier poem 'Home Town'. In the poem I imagine her routine, as she had described it, & imagine the scene—though I've never seen it—as it might be painted, by various artists. Richard Estes & Ralph Goings are American New Photo-Realist painters.
- *Poem (Dynamic Sleeper)*:—was it Rochester or Lord Byron who wrote a poem using a lover's back for support? Or Sedley or

Buckingham? *Scenes of Life at The Capital* is a book-length poem by Philip Whalen.

- *Mostly Hindley Street*—mentions Laurie Duggan & Cath Kenneally; artists Richard Grayson, Simone Hockley; & musician 'Crab' (Graig Tidswell)—of various bands: Speedboat, Crab's Cocktail Hour, The Tuesday Welders, Soulpower, The Hip Replacements, Hipsters in Paradise & others.
- *News Of The Day*: "too-too, too much"—from a song of the same name that the live Velvet Underground album, *1969*, has combined with another, 'Sweet Bonnie Brown'; '(Ain't Never Had) Too Much Fun'—an old song—I know only the Commander Cody version; 'Sweet Jane'—the Velvet Underground; "straight against the light I cross" is from a Frank O'Hara poem.
- *(Two Portraits)*—reports my idle comparison of Tony Towle, a poet I admire greatly, & painter Chuck Close, whose life & work I know little of. The form is two sestinas, linked at the 'envoi' stanza of the first. Other artists mentioned probably don't (for the poem's purposes) require identification.
- *Three poems for John Forbes.* These were written a few months after John died in early 1998.
- *Your Being Away*: the O'Hara poem—from which are taken the quotes my poem so obscurely structures itself around—is 'Those Who Are Dreaming'.
- *American Friends*: *The American Friend* is the movie treatment of a Patricia Highsmith 'Ripley' novel. Set in Germany, the film stars Bruno Ganz—with Dennis Hopper as 'the American friend'.
- *Horizon*—refers to Meaghan Morris's essay 'On The Beach', collected in her book *Too Soon, Too Late*, Indiana University Press. Her essay, in part, considers 'the ordinary'—as it figures in John Forbes, Les Murray & Donald Horne. "I live above a dyke bar" is from Frank O'Hara.
- *Catching Up With Kurt Brereton*: Ardath was a cigarette brand of

my early childhood—not that *I* smoked them: red packet with a small cat as logo I think, or was that the oddly named Craven 'A'? I thought them sophisticated.

- *Traffic Noises, Cups, Voices*: The 'Cone Of Silence' features in some episodes of *Get Smart*, whose hero was Maxwell Smart; Dr Peabody was a professorial, cartoon 'dog' (who wore glasses & expounded confidently & 'equably' on history)—the 'Way Back Machine' allowed him to visit significant moments in the past. Gilligan & Maynard G Krebbs were played by Bob Denver (in, respectively, *Gilligan's Island* & *The Many Loves of Dobie Gillis*).
- *Long Distance Information*: 'Down In Blackbottom'—Joe Evans, recorded in 1931. Stendhal was many times in Rome but much of his Guide to Rome (tho amusing) was fraudulent.
- *Holden Song*: One of Murray Bail's novels, I thought, was *Holden's Song*. But I am wrong, it was *Holden's Performance*.
- *Amaze Your Friends*: The film *Mouchette* is from 1967 & directed by Bresson. The Wayne Shorter tunes referred to are rather restrained &—within his oeuvre & for the time—conservative, but I like them. Tex Perkins is okay by me. Barney Fife was the deputy in *The Andy Griffith Show* & played by Don Knotts. Gomer Pyle: the character from the show of that name, played by Jim Nabors.
- *Hindley Street Today*: the poem begins by echoing the beginning of Ted Berrigan's poem 'Peace'.
- *The Misfits*—a movie starring Eli Wallach & Thelma Ritter. But here it refers to a bunch of poems either very recent or unaccountably strayed from earlier collections, misfits.
- *Some Thinking*: Wally Pater's great line, about the arts & music; Cassavetes, a film director & actor; Fantin-Latour, a painter, often of flowerpieces, in late 19th century Paris; the O'Hara poem referred to is 'The Day Lady Died'; 'Soul Eyes' exists in two versions by John Coltrane, by far the better on a release called *Interplay for Two Trumpets and Two Tenors*.

- *Roman Letters*—were sent to Pam Brown, in Rome, in the same Australia Council studio I had occupied, a few years previous. To some degree the poem responds to remarks made in letters & poems exchanged between Pam, Laurie Duggan & me (some published in our 2005 Vagabond Press book, *Let's Get Lost*).
- *(Pinkham)*: Albert Pinkham Ryder—the American painter, recommended to me by Gregory O'Brien.